MAGO'S DREAM

Also by Ilchi Lee

Healing Society Trilogy

Healing Society: A Prescription for Global Enlightenment
The 12 Enlightenments for Healing Society (June, 2002)
Peaceology for Healing Society (Spring, 2003)

Brain Respiration: Making Your Brain Creative, Peaceful,
and Productive
Dahnhak: The Way to Perfect Health
The Way to Light Up Your Divinity

Unchain Your Soul through

MAGO'S DREAM

Communing with the Earth's Soul

Ilchi Lee

Healing Society

Healing Society

Cover design by il sun Hwang
Illustration by Jong Rin Choi

Healing Society, Inc.
7664 W. Lake Mead Blvd. #109
Las Vegas, NV 89128

e-mail: healingsociety@newhuman.org
Web site: www.healingsociety.org

If you are unable to order this book from your local bookseller,
you may order directly from the publisher.
Call 1-877-324-6425, toll-free.

ISBN 0-9720282-0-X

Printed in South Korea

This book is dedicated to all the members and students
who have put their trust in me through good times and bad,
held together only by their trust and belief
in the inherent goodness of humanity and love for the Earth.

Contents

MAGO'S DREAM

Feeling the Earth's Soul at Sedona Mago Garden

I am standing in Sedona Mago Garden, located about two hours north of Phoenix, Arizona. This is the breathtakingly beautiful land that has given me not only countless hours of indescribable appreciation for the Earth's beauty, but has also inspired me to feel more deeply the meaning of 'Earth' and 'Earth-Human.' Standing here, one can feel the reality of our Earth as it rushes into mind and soul.

Sedona is traditionally sacred land of the Native American tribes in this part of the world, and has been prophesied to be "... a land which will become the center of the coming age by bringing people together in the spirit of peace and reconciliation." Citizens of this beautiful region often speak of Sedona as a sacred land that will herald the coming of a new spiritual civilization where a worldwide spiritual-cultural movement will find its grandest flowering.

From my first encounter with the land, to its current incarnation as 'Sedona Mago Garden,' I have felt indescribable joy and hope, alternating with dark doubts and anxiousness that accurately mirror my history with this piece of heaven on Earth. I first came to the United States in 1993, to introduce the system of Dahnhak and Brain Respiration, a comprehensive system of holistic exercises designed to improve physical, mental, and spiritual health by utilizing the flow of 'Ki' energy, or life energy. This system is already a huge success in Korea.

The first thing I did after landing in America was to buy a used car. I then drove across the continental United States, from NYC to LA, and back again. I even stopped in several Canadian cities including Vancouver and Toronto. Although I had the goal of observing and becoming accustomed to the geography and everyday culture of North America, I was also scanning the terrain for a uniquely 'spiritual' land. In Korea, I had similarly crossed the land several times over, until I chanced upon such a place. I purchased it and made it into a renowned retreat center for spiritual reflection. I was positive that I would find such a place in North America, but it was yet hidden from my eyes.

Mysterious Land of Sedona, Mysterious Soul of Bell Rock

I first encountered mention of the place called Sedona in a local newspaper in 1995, and I instinctively knew that this must be the place I was looking for. I still recall the vivid joy that I felt the first time I drove down to Sedona from Flagstaff; the magical unveiling of the red rocks as they lay stretched out in the distance. It was as if a gorgeous silk-screen painting had descended from the heavens above, with even the trees and shrubs that lined the road-way overflowing with delightful and pure energy. The beauty of this place was sacred; a magnificent red cloth of earth inlaid with beautiful gemstones of pines and cedars, embracing the deepest and bluest sky, gently decorated by soft whispers of white clouds. A spontaneous outcry of joyful recognition arose in me as an inner prayer of deep thanks vibrated throughout my body. Genuine thanks, to the Creator, for allowing such unspeakable beauty to continue to exist. This was the place I had been seeking for. This was my soul's home.

There are twenty-one known energy vortex areas in the world, and Sedona has four of them concentrated within its borders. An energy vortex is a place where an especially high concentration of the earth's energy is channeled toward the earth's surface. A vortex has the effect of helping to restore energy balance in life forms near its source. Of the four vortices in Sedona, the strongest and the most famous is the Bell Rock, a large red rock formation that looks like a bell sprouting from the ground. It looks uniform and gives off an air of safety and security from any angle. A sensitive person can feel a palpable geyser of energy pouring out from Bell Rock to envelop all of Sedona.

I used to climb Bell Rock several times in a single day, attracted by its magical energy and a very familiar sense of kinship, reveling in the current of inspiration that flowed over me. I did not need an excuse to climb its steep and rough hills. I climbed because it was dawn, because it was daylight, because it was twilight, and because the moon was full, half, or crescent. I climbed at the break of day, under the hot afternoon rays of the sun, and even in the blackness of night with coyotes baying at the moon. I was able to place my awareness in this current of rising energy and travel to the four corners of the Earth.

Because of the energy concentration in Bell Rock, many people experience de ja' vu or meet spiritual entities within its immediate sphere of influence. There are research studies underway to explain these paranormal encounters and experiences in terms of the peculiar geological formation of Sedona's ground.

One morning I was on top of Bell Rock in deep meditation. When I meditated, it wasn't unusual for me to see apparitions of people who had lived in these regions many ages ago, including a myriad of entities in Native American guise. However, this day I was visited by the apparition of a kind-looking, elderly, white gentleman with a very soft smile. He did not say anything, but instead, gazed at me in a very non-threatening, and non-burdensome fashion. Thinking that he was just a part of the spiritual panorama unfolding around me, I closed my eyes again and sank into deep awareness. Then he reappeared and approached me in a conscious manner, very unusual in such cases. Feeling that he wanted to speak, I said, "If you have anything to say to me, please go ahead." And he replied, "Welcome to Sedona. I am the spirit of a person who came here to teach about thirty-five years ago. I died only two years ago." As soon as he spoke, a whole new scene started to unfurl in front of me, a moving picture of a wide expanse of striking red earth with small trees and shrubs dotting the landscape. "I have a large area of land in the vicinity of Sedona that I have used as a retreat center. I know that the destiny of the land dictates that it become the center of a new spiritual civilization. I also know that the ultimate realization of this destiny is not with me, but with an awakened soul from the Far East. Please take this land and use it in accordance with its grand destiny." The apparition then faded quickly as the moving picture of the land disintegrated into a brief glimpse of various people arguing loudly, and then, that too faded away.

As soon as I came down from Bell Rock, I resolved to find out if what the old man had said was true, and I headed straight to Sedona's top realtor. I gave him a rough description of the land that I had seen just minutes before, and asked him if he knew of a retreat center in the

Bell Rock

Sedona area.

He replied that he certainly knew of such a place, and that he was the real estate agent of record for that particular piece of property. We set out immediately and drove for about forty minutes from the center of Sedona, along an unpaved and rough road, until we came to a wide expanse of land, of about 150 acres, that lay nestled in the middle of national forest preserve. Rows of small housing units, half hidden by red earth, and blending in perfectly, were very harmonious with the land. The agent explained that all of the buildings of the retreat center were designed by a student of Frank Lloyd Wright to be unobtrusive and 'nature friendly'. From every angle, red rocks piercing the blue sky formed a stunningly beautiful background. Below, the land was a desert forest of cedar trees and cactus plants comprising national forest.

I was given a tour of the property, not only of the land, but also of the dilapidated, but curiously appealing, housing units where visitors and guests had once stayed. The guide asked me whether I was curious about whom the founder of this retreat center was and handed me a book that the man had written. I was shocked, for as soon as I glanced at the cover, I recognized the author's face, with the same expression, and gentle smile I had seen on top of Bell Rock. I asked the guide to tell me the story of the retreat center in greater detail.

The Story of Lester Levenson

The founder's name was Lester Levenson. He had died one years ago in 1994, on the very land on which I was standing. He was originally from New York, a physicist by training, and a very successful businessman. However, in 1952, at the age of 42, he had a second heart attack and was rushed to an emergency room. Although he survived the attack, his doctor sent him home, telling him that there was nothing that the hospital could do for him. It was a death sentence, ameliorated only by the fact that he could die at his home, within a few months or the next time a heart attack struck.

Filled with anger and despair, Lester Levenson was forced to look back and examine every part, every single moment of his life, thinking seriously of suicide several times. However, as the inevitability of death slowly faded from his immediate reality, he realized that he was still breathing, and still a thinking being with nothing to lose.

So he decided to try an experiment with his body, emotions, and consciousness. As he sat quietly in his home, deeper questions about life appeared before him, commanding his attention.

"What is life?" "What am I looking for?" The first answer that rose to his mind was 'happiness.' He then asked himself, "When did I feel most happy?" The answer that first came to him was, "When I received love," but he knew that was untrue. Although he had had many lovers, friends, and family members who loved him, he was not always happy. Therefore, he applied his power of analysis to examination of all the moments of genuine happiness in his life. He finally concluded that he felt genuinely happy only when he had given love to others.

He then asked, "If the moments of unhappiness in my life were the result of my heart not being filled with the giving spirit of love, then might I not turn back the clock in my mind and fill those moments with love, transforming them into happiness?" If happiness was an emotion generated by his state of mind, he surmised he could indeed transform the unhappy moments in his life into happy ones.

He immediately recalled his most recent, unhappy

experience. It was the time when he was told by his doctor to go home to, basically, wait for death. Although he had previously felt rage at the doctor for forcing him to go home, thinking that perhaps the doctor did not want a patient to die on him while in his care, Lester Levenson now thought about how very difficult it must have been for the doctor to tell him that he was certainly going to die. The important thing now was whether he could transform the anger that he had previously felt for the doctor into love. He tried his best to recall those moments of rage and despair and melt them away second by second, moment by moment... until eventually he succeeded in replacing the anger with love. He realized, at that immediate moment, that he was indeed happy.

His experiment continued. For three months, the amount of time he was allotted to live, he sat in his home and brought up every single face, every possible moment of his life, one by one, to dissolve any associated negative emotions that he had had. As he concentrated on his efforts his heart overflowed with the energy of love and joy.

The most difficult thing to do was to face his fear of death. By realizing that the fear of death lay at the root of

Sedona Mago Garden

all negative emotions, he was able to open his heart wide and burn away his fear of death with the flame of his newly recovered love. By being able to let go of every attachment that he had ever held, Lester Levenson was able to let go of his attachment even to life itself and overcome the barrier of fear.

Once his fear of death dissolved, his body felt as light as a feather and he was certain that the disease had left him. Three months after his death sentence, he felt an indescribable feeling of joy, which soon led him into a world of quiet inner peace. In this world of inner peace, that alternately soothed and energized him, he realized that his current physical manifestation as 'Lester Levenson' was not his deepest and truest identity... he was not his body or his thoughts. He was something far deeper, that went to the source of all life, a 'beingness' that was eternal.

Wanting to share what he had learned, he traveled to speak at seminars and to small spiritual minded groups of people. Soon, people flocked to hear his amazing and inspirational story, and his audience swelled to several hundreds and thousands of people.

In 1958, he felt a sudden urge to head west, perhaps

to California. On his way to San Diego, he passed through Arizona and spotted a sign that read 'Sedona'. He heard an inner voice tell him "go there!" Guided by this inner voice, he went immediately to Sedona and was overpowered and overwhelmed by the unique combination of breathtaking beauty and spiritual energy he found there. He decided to purchase land in a remote area of Sedona on which to establish a meditation and retreat center. Here he told people of his experiences and shared the methods by which they too might experience the realization that he had. This eventually became known as the 'Sedona Method.'

The 'Sedona Method' of meditation became known all over the world, with thousands of people practicing its techniques. His closest students in New York visited him often in Sedona, with some of them moving to be near him. One of them was Dr. David Hawkins, the renowned author of *Power vs. Force*, who worked with Nobel Prize winning physicist Linus Pauling. Lester Levenson, who expected to die at the age of 42, lived until he was 84, and was active until the end of his life.

Non-Coincidental Coincidences

Such was the grand story of the land I was looking at for the first time in the searing heat of Sedona's summer day. I was deeply impressed by the story of Lester Levenson and felt a close kinship. His suffering and fear, awakening and enlightenment seemed like they were my own. I was, however, most surprised to hear what he said just before he died: "Soon, an awakened soul from the East will come to use this land to awaken many other souls. I am simply the person who is preparing this land for his arrival."

Although there was controversy surrounding the ownership of the land even while Lester Levenson was alive, he didn't will it to anyone, not even his closest students. When I first went there on that fateful day, it had been two years since his passing and the ownership issue was headed to the courts with several different claims to the land by his numerous students.

As I looked at the expanse of land from a hilltop, I recalled what Lester Levenson's soul had said to me a few hours before. He had said that he wanted me to use the land for my spiritual purposes. No matter how inspiring and 'right' his message felt, however, there was no way this could happen in any realistic sense. "It's all well and good to tell me to use this land, but it's another thing for me to actually attempt to buy it. We simply do not have the financial wherewithal to afford this... and what if we do acquire it? It's a huge piece of land in the middle of the Arizona desert. Even Americans failed to operate this retreat center in the black... what can we as Koreans do? We don't have any business foundation in America and we don't even speak English well..." Such were my thoughts as I considered the message I had received from the gentleman on Bell Rock, a combination of hope, doubt, and wry humor. "Although I know that Lester Levenson is a sincere soul, how can I be sure that his message is true? I wish that he had been more specific about the land and its possibility for future use... a map to a nearby buried treasure wouldn't hurt, either."

On that day, I had no choice but to turn back, and I decided to forget about the land. However, whenever I meditated, Lester Levenson's soul would come to visit me, gazing at me in silence and with a certain longing, before disappearing. When I told him that it was not realistically possible for me to take over his retreat center, he would just circle around and gaze at me with a look of sad hope. Soon he started to appear in my dreams, and I decided to go back once more to see the land where once a thriving retreat center had stood. Lost in my thoughts and the mesmerizing beauty of the land, I took a long, leisurely walk along its many trails. I encountered a small and neglected grave, seemingly lost among the wild desert grasses. The headstone indicated that here laid Lester Levenson. In a moment of piercing empathy, I felt the sweat and tears that he must have shed to create and fulfill his vision on this patch of Earth. I felt the overflowing love, the weariness and the loneliness.

I was forced to reconsider my previous decision. Should I risk everything I had built up over the past 15 years to purchase a large piece of land in the middle of an enchantingly beautiful but foreboding desert, because of the power of the entreaties of a pure soul? All of my closest colleagues and students tried to dissuade me. In the following months, I visited the land several more times, always with the nagging and momentous question of, "Should I, or should I not?"

Then one day, I read in the local newspaper that the land of the late Lester Levenson would be put up for public auction to pay off the legal fees that had accrued as a result of the long legal conflict among his students over ownership of the land. Now, I was out of time. I had to buy the land or let it go forever. I decided to visit one last time before making a final decision.

As was the case with each previous visit, I was overwhelmed by the surrounding scenery and powerful energy of the land, while saddened by the gradual state of disrepair and neglect of the retreat center. As I once again walked up to Lester Levenson's gravesite, the tall unkempt sea of wild grass greeted me with an undulating sway. A fierce wind blew, kicking the red dry dirt up in a swirl, almost as if the land itself was crying out for love and hope of a new incarnation. I stopped as I felt the heart of the land beating its own sadness. Suddenly a powerful tremor rumbled underneath my feet, accompanied by an inner voice that cried out resoundingly, "Will you truly forsake me?"

A jolt of electricity went through me as every cell in my body responded to the call of the land with a cry equal in power and longing. "Is this what you truly want of me?" Just then, incredibly, a bolt of lightening struck only a few feet from where I was rooted, crackling with unseen heat as dry dirt spewed violently into the air. Shaken by the experience, I stumbled to the ground, on my knees in implicit submission, "I shall do what you ask..."

Yet, no matter how truthful or powerful a message is, one is nevertheless confronted with doubts and fear for the future, when the path, logically followed, appears to lead to certain failure and ruin. However, when the message comes from the source of life, then you have no choice but to accept it, however impossible it may seem at the time. There is no other option.

After many tribulations and complications, the purchase of the land was finally effected by a non-profit organization whose mission is to engage in furthering the cause of peace in the world through human consciousness raising projects-thus, Sedona Mago Garden was born after many months of labor pains.

From Mago's Heart Comes the Inspiration

A slew of obstacles and difficulties lay in front us as we attempted to operate the retreat center, all the more so because we did not have an operational plan in place before purchasing the land. However, I experienced first hand, how the spiritual inspiration of the land was able to weave its magical destiny into reality.

In May of 1999, I hosted a lecture-event called 'Meeting with the Creator' with Neale Donald Walsch, the worldwide best selling author of the *Conversations with God* books, which have been translated into 27 languages. I had received inspiration for this event while meditating in Sedona Mago Garden and had invited the world famous author to participate. He was fortuitously holding his own workshop at Sedona Mago Garden the same week. Several hundred people from both America and Korea attended, and I not only gained an invaluable friend in Neale, but also he offered to publish my book in the USA. The book, *Healing Society*, came out about a year and a half later and shot straight to the top of Amazon.com's overall sales ranking within a month of publication.

Neale and I confirmed in each other a mirror image of our spiritual vision and commitment to humanity. We have since co-established the 'New Millennium Peace Foundation' and hosted the 'First Annual Humanity Conference'. World famous thinkers participated in the conference and drafted the first ever 'Declaration of Humanity', demonstrating agreement with and support for a worldwide spiritual-cultural movement for peace. This is discussed in greater detail in a later chapter.

In Sedona Mago Garden, I was also inspired to form the 'World Earth-Human Alliance', a non-profit cooperative networking organization for non-governmental organizations seeking to use the powers of innate human spirituality to heal our current divisions and create a lasting and equitable world peace.

Sedona Mago Garden is the land of the Mother Earth, providing an infinite source of creative inspiration. Anyone who sets foot here to gaze upon the rising and setting of the sun will feel the sacredness of the land. As twilight flows over the backdrop of the amazing beauty of the cliffs and mountains adorned with Sedona ruby red, you will surely experience the touch of the Earth's soul, Mago. With each flower I plant and each tree I water here in Sedona Mago Garden, I feel myself intimately joined to the land as my heart beats in rhythm to the heart of the Earth. And here in Sedona Mago Garden, I work to realize my life long mission as an Earth-Human to help others feel the joy of the unbreakable bond that their souls share with Mago's soul.

How Does Peace Come?

Since I have never orbited the Earth, I have not seen the Earth in her entirety. However, I know that the Earth is absolutely stunning in her beauty, not because I have seen the photos taken from space, but because I know that she is the source and the root of all life, as we know it. How can she be anything less than beautiful? I eat, breathe, and live because the Earth so graciously allows me to.

I am not a geologist familiar with all the wonderful details of Earth's make up, nor am I an ardent environmental activist courageous enough to block bulldozers from removing trees with my own body. However, I am deeply aware that I exist only because the Earth exists. I am also someone who has spent all of my adult life examining ways in which we may achieve world peace. I am doing my best to contribute to its realization. Above all else, I am someone who can feel the energy and soul of the Earth. I can feel the sadness and grief that the Earth feels as she watches her children destroy themselves along with her. I feel the Earth's soul quiver, not with fear and anger at the destruction wrought by humanity, but with the concern and love that she holds for all of life, in her bosom. I write this book to share the soul of the Earth as I feel her everyday.

I believe that the two most important focal points for all of humanity in the 21st century are the Earth, and the human brain. The health of the Earth is the only standard that is all encompassing enough to overcome the ethnic, cultural, religious, and national boundaries that are rending the world asunder. This alone can bring humanity together under a common system of life values, while preserving the wonderful traditions of the various peoples of the world in their spectacular diversity. Only the Earth can become the central axis around which world peace can be spun, for no religion is more compelling, no nation larger, and no peoples older than the Earth herself.

For that to happen, the collective human consciousness must expand and advance to the point where our highest common identification is as Earth-Humans, first and foremost, before we pigeonhole ourselves into different national, ethnic, and religious categories. This advance in human consciousness can only be achieved through the human brain. This is why the human brain is so crucial in the peace equation.

My talk about the importance of the Earth is certainly not new. Many people have worked very diligently to educate the rest of us about the dangers threatening the environment. To my eternal admiration and appreciation, they have spent their lives furthering the cause of the preservation of the Earth. Efforts are being made to publicize the importance of insuring sustainability of economic expansion by balancing the needs of human civilization with that of the ecosystem. However, I wish to talk about the Earth not as a network of constantly varying ecosystems, but as the root of our existence, the central standard bearer of our collective life values, and the source of all life that calls her home. I believe that it is just as crucial to feel the reality of the Earth, as it is to understand her disparate components on an intellectual level. Only then will our intellectual understanding gain power and be transformed into action.

The important thing is to build a bridge between our soul and the soul of the Earth. For this to occur, we must know the Earth not only on a material plane, but also on a spiritual one. We have to realize that the Earth herself is a living entity. With her unique energy and soul, she is capable of communicating with and nurturing the innumerable forms of life that populate her being. By feeling the soul of the Earth, I have been awakened to the

Oneness of all life. The more people communicate with the soul of the Earth, experientially realize this Oneness, and socially actualize its consciousness-expanding consequences, the quicker will we achieve lasting peace on Earth.

It is my hope that my book, *Peaceology*, can be said to present a comprehensive philosophy and specific ways to actualize peace, and I hope that *Mago's Dream* will be a guide that will lead you into an awe-inspiring and deeply comforting experience of bonding with the soul of the Earth, 'Mago.'

You probably already know that all people of the world are brothers and sisters in our common human heritage, which cannot be broken by transitory barriers of ethnicity, religion, and nationhood. This is obvious to everyone. However, this knowledge itself has proven to be sorely deficient in effecting fundamental and lasting change. We need to understand this in a way that will shake us to the core of our being, and lift us from our lack of consciousness in a blinding swirl of enlightenment. Only then will our brains undergo a fundamental transformation, translate the knowledge into action, and change the world for the better. Meeting with 'Mago' will lead you to such understanding.

As a brother to a brother, a sister to a sister, a parent to a child, and a child to a parent, I offer you my soul, my life, my all, knowing that we share the common destiny of our collective creation. And as one Earth-Human to another, I salute you in our common spiritual heritage and love of the Earth.

Ilchi Lee
Sedona, Arizona
February 15th, 2002

Earth

Life is a trip, not in a metaphorical sense but literally. We are all taking a trip through the universe on a spaceship called, 'Earth.' Our souls dropped onto the fertile plains of Earth and we became passengers, not knowing our point of origin or our destination, almost as if we were unwilling and unaware participants in a cosmic bungee jump. What we do know, however, is that this trip is a journey of growth, both for our individual souls and for the collective soul of humanity. These are not separate.

Life is a trip, but not an endless one, or idyllic. I am sometimes surprised by my sense of urgency when I think of the direction in which humanity and Earth are headed. Burning whispers hiss in my ear from every direction. "We really don't have time..." "This is not the way..." "We can't go on like this..." We, as humanity, are collectively feeling the critical nature of our situation. We are both bewildered and panicked, looking for a leader, a Messiah, who will lead us out of our current Egypt, only to fall back into mounting despair as we are repeatedly disappointed. A journey can be described as a trip only when you know the destination. If not, a journey is only aimless wandering.

The Earth Can Bring Us Together

By most accounts, the Earth is five billion years old and the oldest ancestors of human beings first appeared on Earth about three million years ago. It has only been 40,000 years since humans began using tools, indicating what was to come. In the 200 years since the beginning of the Industrial Revolution, no corner of Earth, however remote, remains safe from the greedy touch of human hands. Always expanding, always profiting, and always hoarding and destroying everything in our path, until we ourselves have come to recognize the cancerous nature of our so called civilized activities. There are currently six billion human beings on Earth. That number is expected to rise to ten billion by 2050. Twelve percent of today's population, 1.2 billion people, are barely surviving on less than one dollar a day. How many will have to get by on one dollar a day 50 years from now? The United Nation's environmental report states that over ninety percent of the world's population will suffer from a water shortage in 25 years. Over four million children are already dying every year from unavailability of water. We now find ourselves living on an Earth from which we are afraid to eat, drink, and breathe. The world's foremost experts tell us that, in spite of degrees of differences, no country in the world is engaged in economic policies that will allow 'sustainable' industrial activities. Just as we realize the importance of health after a bout with a serious disease, we are only now realizing the preciousness of the Earth and the environment, as the signs of distress become more evident and urgent.

We can choose our religion. We can choose our citizenship. We can even choose our gender nowadays. However, we cannot choose the planet we live on. We

cannot choose, or not choose, the Earth. We can live without religion, without countries, and even without supermarkets. We cannot live without the Earth. Earth is the Mother of all life, as we know it, UFO proponents notwithstanding. Her gifts and love are plentiful and unconditional, but, unless we change course, neither will last much longer. It is only a matter of common sense and reasonable responsibility for children to care for an ailing parent. What will we choose to do, now that we know that our actions are harming our mother? And who can give us the guidance to choose wisely? As they say, Mom always knows best...

Today, people and their money are not bound by national boundaries or cultural traditions. They go wherever they please, binding the Earth into an ever-tightening knot of a global village. Our quandary lies in that the more plentiful and advanced our material civilization becomes, the more empty and anxious our hearts feel. Many of us have lost our way, wandering in a spiritual wasteland, filled with meaningless routines that are inherently unsatisfying and draining. We are lost and without a compass to provide consistent direction, without a system of life values for humanity to share collectively.

Our general confusion is evident in the breakdown of traditional social order in family, nation, and religion. Divorce rates approach fifty percent in most industrialized countries, rapidly making the traditional family model obsolete. Feeling restricted by national borders, arguments for a multi-national citizenship are gaining merit and support. Churches and temples no longer fill the deep spiritual hunger of youth, and congregations slowly but surely diminish to gatherings of the old faithful. Our traditional values and morals are slowly losing their once absolute authority, necessitating creation of a larger and wider system of values that can guide us in this rapidly changing and expanding age.

We are at a very critical point on our journey.

At this point, when our old system of values seems devoid of content and power, will we break apart into disparate components? Will we seek only to fulfill our individual needs through competition and domination, without regard to the whole? Are we no longer able to share collective values, or a collective dream? Will we stay chained to protecting and satisfying our 'selves' in isolation? Or will we once again feel the joy of a shared dream and shared achievement? Is this the best that we can do?

Is this the life we want? These are fiercely compelling questions, and clamor for our attention.

Our intellectual and deepest spiritual wisdom tells us that this is not so. Our joy and my joy, our soul and my soul, our destiny and my destiny are not mutually exclusive but inherently interdependent. We can all revolve around the sun as one united entity while rotating within our own world of joy and satisfaction. One need not be exclusive of the other. We must find a central standard of value that can overcome the differences among the scattered systems of values that drive the world's human societies into conflict with one another. We need a central and comprehensive system of 'living' values that can unite humanity under one umbrella, while preserving and even celebrating our diversity. That will allow us to rotate individually while we revolve collectively. Where can we find such a standard?

Earth. It has always been with us.

The Earth is the common, central value around which we can rally, the root of our existence, the actual reality of our lives. No truth we seek, nor values we live by, can exist without the Earth. No gods can exist without the Earth. In Neil Gaiman's exquisite novel, *American Gods*, a buffalo-man, symbolizing the land, speaks thus when referring to both humans and gods: " ...they never understood that they were here, and that the people who worshipped them were here ... because it suited us that they be here. But we can change our minds. And perhaps we will." Only Earth can act as the standard bearer that can gather and lead our collective human consciousness to the next plane.

Our souls are clamoring, not for the 'peace of separateness' belonging to a particular religion, nation, or people, and separating us into losers and winners, but for the 'peace on Earth', that can be celebrated by all life on Earth. We will know true peace when we all realize that the Earth is the final arbitrator of life and that the 'Earth-Human' is our highest common identity as human beings.

Why Does Peace Fight against Peace?

Peace has been a goal and a dream of every leader, every civilization, every nation, and every government ever to exist in recorded history. And yet, the twentieth century saw two world wars of unprecedented death and destruction, violent revolutions that uprooted and marginalized tens of millions, lesser wars that nevertheless killed and maimed millions more, and an unimaginable program of mass murder that targeted a group of people for reasons that were totally unjustifiable and horrific in their twisted logic. As I write these words, the world continues on with its destructive legacy of war. However, every leader or general who is engaged in this brutal continuation of war is fighting for the cause of justice and peace. 'A war to end all wars...' Indeed.

Until now, the chief mainstays of the human value system have been the categories of nation, religion, and ethnicity. In the name of these categories, groups of people have engaged in an endless cycle of war and conflict in order to secure 'freedom, justice, and peace' for their own particular group. The 'freedom, justice, and peace' gained in these wars is prejudicial by nature, and has always been achieved at the sacrifice of another group or groups. The consequence of this has been an endless and vicious cycle of retribution. All in the name of 'freedom, justice, and peace.'

All civilizations outlaw the killing of one individual by another and punish the perpetrator with the most severe form of punishment possible. However, all civilizations praise and reserve high honors for those who kill others in the heat of battle. If the war is a religious one, then the best killers are not only the bravest but also the holiest, with a place reserved in heaven for them, secured by the blood of the enemies of the 'one true god'.

When I observe the group egotism that has spawned so many wars and so much destruction, I cannot help but wonder whether much of our brilliant material advancement is motivated in part, or in whole, by the desire of the various groups to become stronger and more powerful. Since winning wars is central to becoming a stronger and more dominating people, we have developed better guns, longer-range artillery, and more efficient means of mass killing. There seems to be no end to human ambition and group egotism.

A crime committed by one individual against another individual for personal gain is punished severely. However, a crime committed by a group, national or religious, is outside of the realm of our current justice system. Therefore, what is history except a story of brute strength, a story made up by the victors to justify their actions against another, weaker, people.

Even religions, crying out for salvation and 'peace on

earth,' are engaged in endless turf wars. What is religion but an amalgam of social values and dogma that favors the needs and ambition of group egotism? Various religious groups have been fighting against one another throughout the history of humankind, all in the name of justice and peace. Often they eradicate all vestiges of another people's culture while simultaneously shouting a message of redeeming love.

Humanity still hasn't learned the basics of forgiveness and peaceful co-existence. How many more victims will we create through brutal acts of injustice perpetrated in the name of justice, peace, and truth? And how many more victims will these victims create in turn? The future is predictable and scary.

The horrific terrorist acts of September 11th, 2001 have shown us that our sense of security, based on economic prosperity and military strength is an illusion. Who would have thought that the most powerful nation in the history of the world, both militarily and economically, would be vulnerable to such acts of wanton destruction? We now have no alternative but to carefully examine the 'pursuit of peace' that we have thus far engaged in. Is it truly effective, and is it truly for peace?

In August 2000, I attended the historic 'Millennium World Peace Summit of Religious and Spiritual Leaders'. 1,200 of the world's preeminent religious and spiritual leaders, representing the majority of the world's faith traditions, gathered at the General Assembly Hall of the United Nations for four days to condemn the use of religion as justification for war, and to come together in a spirit of harmony and mutual respect. This is all well and good.

However, when the conference was over, the head office of one of the three major religions of the world issued a statement to the effect that, "although it recognizes the right of other religions to exist, it nevertheless remains firm in its' belief that it is the only religion that will guarantee true salvation." This is akin to saying, "You can live your way, but you won't be living correctly unless you live like we do, since we know that we know better than you".

What is this but an invitation to battle, if not on a battlefield, at least in the hearts of men and women? This kind of doctrine eventually leads to real bloodshed, as history has proven time and time again. Such is the limitation of current religious systems and their complicity in perpetuating continuing crimes against humanity. Notwithstanding the many positive contributions that religions have made to civilization, they cannot lead us to 'peace on Earth' because they are inherently prejudicial... dividing rather than unifying.

It is now time to acknowledge the ultimate and core value that is capable of encompassing and superceding the partial and prejudicial orientation of the current value systems of the world. It is the one that can become a fulcrum point that will allow balance, harmony, and peaceful co-existence of all people. This is the Earth. The Earth cannot be claimed by any one group or organization regardless of its size or power. If humanity can be said to share one collective vision, it would be peace on Earth. This collective vision may also be our only hope for survival in the very near future. To realize that we are all Earth-Humans... this is the key.

The Earth from the Outside In and the Inside Out

With the advances in communications technology and widespread travel, the Earth has indeed become smaller, more familiar, and more intimate. This is all the more amazing because we didn't even know that the Earth was round or orbited around the sun until a few hundred years ago. However, with advances in science, we have acquired more and more knowledge about the Earth. We have all seen pictures of the Earth taken from outer space, and we are able to point out approximately where we live and were born on this cosmic sphere of beautiful colors, suspended in the magical darkness of the universe.

As children, we are taught that the Earth revolves around the sun as the third planet of the solar system, knowledge that Galileo had to risk his life to defend. As transportation has developed, we have further realized that what we hold to be true and inviolate in one part of the world is not necessarily true in another part. Humans have created a world of omnipresent relativity in everything from social values to cultural rituals. Studies in geology and biology have awakened us to the incredible history and living processes of Earth, from erupting volcanoes and sliding plates, to the mind numbing variety of life that she nurtures, creates, and destroys... only to create again with a love and patience that only a mother could have. But have we ever seen the Earth from the Earth's point of view? Have we felt the Earth as she herself must feel?

With our minds, let us travel outward into the cosmos, until we are looking down at the Earth. Free your awareness from the time and space continuum and see the Earth in a state of absolute freedom. See the blue green sphere, magically suspended in inky, all-encompassing blackness, soft and bright in her soothing luminosity.

Do you see the assorted and indescribable colors weaving in and out of this earthly tapestry? Can you see the different colored petals of flowers as they sway in the wind, weaving and twirling, mixing with the wild grasses to go forth as a living breeze, only to fall onto the dark soil as an invisible mist of green life? Do you see the dynamic beauty of animals as they prowl, swallowed by the protective green gauze of the forests or the harsh yellow tint of the desert? Do you see any differences in human beings in terms of their skin color, body types, or any other criteria that you can think of?

Of course you do, for life is an expression of infinite creativity. No living thing is identical to any other living thing, even among the same species. And do you realize that this is a blessing, the greatest ever, and that 'sameness' is unnatural and an affront to life? Life is not an imitation, but an unending process of original creation.

Can you now feel an overwhelming burst of inspiration and gratitude for this infinite variety? For the love of the Creator, as life is bursting in full bloom in its blinding and brash beauty?

Look again. Do you see any borders disfiguring the striking jigsaw puzzle of the landmasses, black lines across the verdant land? Do you see any fences separating the blue seas from the emerald forests? Can you sense any discord or a cacophony of jarring colors in this canvas of life called 'Earth?' Do you now see the magical harmony created from the miracle of diversity and differences? Do you now realize that diversity and differences are to be celebrated rather than grudgingly acknowledged? Good, you have now glimpsed the life that is Earth!

Earth does not have borders, whether national, religious, or ethnic. Why should she try to keep the diversity of life, which is itself the essence of creation, separated and imprisoned, preventing her from fulfilling her divine right to blend and add another layer of life to the heavenly canvas? Then why are we humans trying to keep ourselves separate and divided? Why are we trying to prevent ourselves from fulfilling our own role as part of life? What's so important about ethnicity, nationality, and the various religions that force us to overlook our inherent right to truly live in the deepest meaning of the word?

If we can all experience the reality of the Earth as we have just done together, we will realize that a simple shift of awareness is all that's needed to solve the seemingly intractable problems facing us today. All we need to do is to allow our awareness to break through the prison bars of false and negative information. They are not real anyway.

When Earth becomes our collective source of life values, then we will realize that the boundaries that we have set for ourselves are unnecessary, that the endless competition driving our society is juvenile, and that our relentless anxiety arises from denial of our true life. When Earth becomes the center of our values, then politics, economics, and even religion will take their rightful place as tools, not masters, of our lives.

This shift of awareness is the most important key to the road to peace. Peace sought by a single nation or a religion will inevitably generate conflict. Only peace centered on and encompassing the whole Earth can lead us to the 'promised land' of ancient, wise lore.

Mago,
Soul of the Earth

In order to achieve genuine peace by placing the Earth at the fulcrum of living values, we need not only understand the importance of the Earth, but also be able to communicate with her in a personal, intimate, and profound way. Even if we all intellectually understand that the Earth is the key to peace, it is for naught if this knowledge is not made tangible and applicable.

In order for information to enter the brain and then be expressed as action, that information must be processed and delivered to the furthest nerve endings and muscles. Similarly, establishment of the Earth as the center of our values must go beyond the intellectual plane and be ingrained into every cell of our bodies in order to be realized.

For this to happen, our hearts must be able to communicate with the heart of the Earth. Although many people realize the importance of the Earth, they only think of the Earth as a large material object, because they don't know how to connect with her heart, thus leaving their hearts barren and lifeless. The moment that you can feel the heart of the Earth and consciously accept it as such, is a moment of enlightenment, for you will have allowed your awareness to meld with that of the Earth and see and feel her as she herself does.

Feeling the Earth's Body, Energy, and Soul

When I think of the Earth, the picture that first comes to my mind is one taken by a satellite from outer space, a blue-green ball tantalizingly covered with wisps of white clouds. To communicate with the Earth's heart, but not only know the Earth on a physical level, but also know her on a spiritual one. It is far more important to be able to feel the wholeness of the Earth than to know her geological history or the correct correlation of her limestone layers.

Have you ever said "Good Morning!" to a stand of particularly tall grass or a wild flower that opened its petals especially early one morning? Anyone who is a gardener has had experiences of talking with the plants under his or her care. When you have an experience of feeling the 'heart' of a plant, you no longer regard the plant as mere decoration, but as an entity of life. In point of fact, you have not actually spoken to the plant in the usual sense, but you have indeed felt and sensed the energy and soul of the life expressed through the shape and form of the plant. Likewise, in order to communicate with the earth, we must come to know Earth as a living entity, with a material body, life energy, and an eternal soul, as all forms of life.

The body of the earth consists of the mountains, seas, rivers, plants, and animals. It is everything that we can see, touch, and feel. Earth is not just a spherical ball of dirt. It includes the atmosphere that surrounds it, the clouds that float above, and the rain that quenches the land. Human beings are, of course, part of the Earth, born and raised by the generosity and bounty of the Earth.

Human beings possess a rational mind, the highest intellectual ability of all animals and plants on earth, gifted with the capability of creating an environment to suit their needs and wants. However, such capability still does not allow human beings to exist outside of the Earth, not even in the foreseeable future.

The Earth continuously pours a tremendous amount of energy into the atmosphere, forming an energy field matrix from which all life draws life-sustaining energy, most commonly in the form of breath. Here, a breast-feeding analogy is appropriate, for we are indeed sucking life-giving nutrition from our Mother Earth every second of our lives. The energy that fills the universe is called Cosmic Energy, (or Chunjikiun in Dahnhak parlance). It constitutes an invisible sea of energy. This is the energy that is the basis of all existence, for even material forms and shapes are part of an ever-changing current of energy. Earth's energy is part of a continuum of Cosmic Energy, (Chunjikiun). Cosmic Energy is the Earth's Energy.

Just as human beings have a heart, so does the Earth. As human beings have a soul, so does the Earth. It is the same heart and soul that gave birth to all life on her land and in her waters. It is the heart and soul of a mother that

is a continuation of the Cosmic Mind, (or Chunjimaeum). Chunjimaeum is cosmic consciousness that forms an awareness matrix over all of the cosmos, through all its dimensions, and is not bound by time or space. It is home to any and all souls as they return from untold journeys and a port to any and all souls as they embark on a new journey. Cosmic Mind is the Earth's Mind.

Mago, the Earth's Soul

Regardless of variations in time, geography, and culture, all civilizations have referred to the Earth as the 'Mother Earth.' Korean tradition refers to the Earth as 'Mago' by combining the roots of two terms. 'Ma, Mater, Umma, Mom,' the almost universal sound for Mother, is combined with 'Go', which signifies ancient or old in traditional Asian writing, to form the word 'Mago'. Directly translated, 'Mago' thus means 'Ancient Mother.' This is not to be confused with an image of an old hag, or witch, a distinctly European invention dating back to Middle Ages. Mago is closer to the Hellenic-Roman concept of earth goddess, Gaiea.

Since the human soul is intimately connected to the

Earth's soul, we can truly feel the Earth in our hearts when we are able to commune with her on a spiritual plane. Only then will we be able to see the Earth with the Earth's awareness, leading to a human culture of harmony and forgiveness. Indigenous Native Americans of Sedona also believed that the Earth had a soul, prophesying that the Earth will only be healed and humans only become complete when we can commune with her soul and seek to protect her body.

Mago is a concept far different, and far older, than the concept of god. Gods are invisible, but Mago is both visible and tangible. We can see, hear, and touch the Mother Earth, the ever-present root of all life on our planet. Until now, humanity has had an on-going and one-sided love affair with various gods, trusting in them to secure and bless our individual nations, peoples, religions, and families, praying endlessly to the divine deaf ear and taking advantage of non-existent pronouncements to justify whatever they wanted. Who could accuse them of being wrong? The gods were never held responsible, nor their messengers accountable. However, since she has both a body and a soul, the Earth can tell us immediately, in a palpable and tangible way, what is and what is not pleasing to her. We cannot conveniently wish her existence away, as we have done with countless gods. Yet, it almost seems as if we are trying in earnest to destroy her and to destroy ourselves in the process. We seem to be attempting to uproot our own existence.

If any love has the forgiveness and patience to guide a wayward child, no, a juvenile delinquent, like humanity, it has to be the love of a Mother. If her love is acknowledged and accepted in its benevolent omnipresence and omniscience, then what other possible decision could we make except to respond in kind? In order for us to effect a shift in human consciousness to a level on which we can have a 'heart-to-heart' conversation with the Earth, and feel her love, we must reopen a channel of communication that we have always had, but have not always been aware of.

Let us reawaken our senses. Let us listen to our Mother. Let us feel her embrace.

Let us.

Reawakening Our Sense of Energy

Although every experience that occurs in the world of the

five human senses is, strictly speaking, an energy experience, you can experience energy directly as three main sensations; a sense of tickling electricity, a sense of the pulling and pushing of a magnetic force, and a sense of heat and cold. When your senses become trained with practice, you begin to have a deep sense of energy as it moves through your mind and body. We can call this the language of the soul. With this you can communicate with all of existence, and fully utilize the information contained within the flow of energy. A sharing of the soul can only occur via communication through energy. Therefore, it is only possible to commune with Mago when we have reawakened our ability to sense energy, which has long remained dormant.

When you can sense the energy, you don't need research studies to tell you that the climate is warming, species are disappearing by the hundreds everyday, and the rain forests are losing ground at an alarming rate. You don't need specific numbers. You can feel the deleterious effects that these have on Earth. Just feel. Feel how the Earth feels. Feel how the sea feels. See how the sky feels. And see how Mago feels.

Energy is the universal language that we humans

must adopt in order to engage in spiritual growth. Energy is the language of the soul that provides the path that will lead you to Earth, to the cosmos, and ultimately, to yourself.

Feeling the Earth's Body

The trees that surround your house, the shiny dew that greets you in the morning, the mountains yonder and the river under the bridge are all manifestations of the Earth's body. Bread, vegetables, and fruits are all products of Earth's body. Water, which composes about seventy percent of our human bodies, flows from the Earth. All life is born, reared, and returned to Earth. We can most palpably sense the 'Motherliness' of the Earth through the embrace of her lands and bounty of her seas. All of nature is her body. Everything from the wisps of clouds in the sky, to the blind worm in the soil, from the deepest of her oceans to the tallest of her peaks, are her organs and cells, to be nurtured and cared for.

Imagine ... and see her again, being blessed by the sun in the day and the moon at night. Have you ever lain in a sunny field of grass, and felt the warm rays of the sun flow through you like so many pine needles? Have you ever watched the golden moon play hide-and-seek with the clouds, wearing a circular aura of majesty in the night-time sky, and illuminating the mysterious silhouette of the lands below? Have you ever stood, trembling in the cold wind, staring at the millions of stars as they twinkle in the moonless, clear night ... so near and yet so far away? These things are all possible because you are standing, with your feet planted firmly upon the Earth, breathing the air, and the energy that she so generously gives.

Breathing in the Earth with a Tree

Everything on Earth is, first and foremost, connected by breath. What we breathe in, others breathe out. What others breathe in, we breathe out. The cycle is repeated endlessly, encircling all forms of life on Earth. We can feel life through our breath. We can also feel our soul through breath. We can feel our own divinity through our breath.

There are two gates through which life enters the human body. One is the nose and the other is the mouth. Invisible air and heaven's energy (ChunKi) enter through the nose. The Earth's energy (JiKi) in the form of food, enters through the mouth. Our lives are sustained by the circulation of heaven's and earth's energy.

Thirty percent of the air we breathe is oxygen. Oxygen comes from trees and plants, which breathe in the carbon dioxide that we breathe out. Trees and humans thus have a symbiotic relationship in life. I would now like to introduce you to a simple meditation that you can do, one that will help you feel the Earth through the life of a tree. This meditation is best done in the outdoors, filled with trees, but it is also possible to practice indoors.

Close your eyes and imagine a tree in front of you, its strong branches packed with healthy leaves and filled with vitality. The oxygen that the tree pumps out comes into our bodies to help generate the energy that allows us to live. Conversely, the energy that we breathe out as carbon dioxide feeds the tree, and helps maintain its life. Feel the air as it enters through your nose and into your body. Feel every particle, every molecule, of the air as it flows through your nose, mouth, and into your lungs, being absorbed by each single cell in your body. Feel the refreshing and literally life-giving pleasure provided by the simple act of inhaling. Now exhale, letting your body relax, newly invigorated.

See the tree again. Feel the tree through your breath. Feel the life of the tree transmitted through the air and communicated through breath. This tree has its roots embedded deep within the earth. From the earth to the tree, from the tree to you, from you back to the tree, the cycle of life and energy can be sensed, not on an imaginative plane, but palpably, in reality. Through this cycle of breathing, the Earth's energy and soul are transmitted to us, showing us that our lives are not separate and isolated, not even for a moment. This interchange of energy is a fundamental function of life at all levels. Breathe with the tree, and you will feel the inescapable oneness that connects us to one other and to the Earth.

I am breathing, as are you. We are creatures whose noses are rooted in the air that we share. We don't have to pay for this privilege. We just breathe. Who, then, is the owner of this air, the most precious of all commodities? If we were to calculate it in terms of money, the sum would literally be priceless. However, we have never been presented with a bill, thank God.

Countless trees sustain our lives. Trees have supplied humanity and other creatures with one's worth of oxygen and energy, thereby life. Trees have never asked to be given credit for this contribution. Trees have never asked to be worshipped for this 'life-giving' activity. Trees have never asked to be recognized in the slightest way. However, if we were to pick something to honor or worship based on merit or contribution to the prosperity of humanity, any old oak or poplar tree would come far before any ideas of god. In fact, a single needle on a cactus in a forsaken desert would qualify before any abstract concept of a god.

Trees heal without having learned any special knowledge or developing any particular religious faith. The Earth supplies the trees with water and nutrition without any conditions. What is more important to us, trees or gods? What is more important to us, Earth or gods? If I were told that trees are gods, and the Earth is a god, then I would be less confused. I cannot believe that any god can be more important than the trees, the air, and the Earth. Nor proscribe to the belief that any god would exist in a vacuum far above, instead of residing within the trees, the forests, and the streams that surround us. Reside within the Earth herself. I believe firmly that 'god' exists within all life that we are witnesses to today and beyond.

Humans and trees have no business dealings in the

normal sense. There are no brokers who take their cut, whose profit is calculated by the amount of air that we consume. We don't need a lawyer, an accountant, or an arbitrator to regulate our dealings with the trees. Therefore, we haven't had a single incident of conflict. No tree has refused us its exhalation of oxygen just as we have never refused a tree our breath of carbon dioxide. The reason why there are no conflicts in this life exchanging process is that there are not any interlopers seeking to take credit for what is not theirs, coveting honors they don't deserve. All conflict arises out of just such misguided self-aggrandizement. However, the real giver of life does not seek any recognition, prayers, or worship. If this is not real love, then what is? If this is not divinity, then what is?

All of life is intimately involved in this cycle. There is no sense in labeling who the giver is or who the taker is. Everybody owes somebody something. I literally owe my life to a plant, tree, or a shrub nearby, not in any metaphysical sense but in a real sense. Ultimately, a tree is a tree, the Earth, and the universe. It is you, it is me, and it is all of humanity. When we realize this, we will treat each other, and nature, as we ourselves would like to be treated.

For a single seed or cone to mature into a healthy tree, you need the full-fledged participation of many factors, including the water, earth, sunlight, and wind. In order to grow, the tree, and all life, opens itself up to these energies. However, we humans often make the mistake of closing ourselves off, while simultaneously trying to attain those things that are crucial to our survival. We live too much in our own world of isolated bubbles, blown from the hot air of self-inflation.

We think that we see because we have eyes. True, but what is more fundamental is that we see because the sun shines from above, providing us with light. We see only because of the reflection of light by material objects. Look at your hand. What do you see? Do you see fingers, five of them? Now look closer. What else do you see? Do you see the empty spaces in between your fingers? How about the stars above? They appear to be separated from each other, sparkling and beautiful in their cold isolation. Yet, do you see the dark space that connects them, suspending them in a sea of eternal blackness?

Sometimes, we need to look beyond the obvious in reality to peer into the truth behind everyday phenomena. All it takes is a change in focus, a simple shift in point of view. Likewise, all it takes for us to see and feel the Earth is a simple realignment of our given senses. Since we are children of Earth, we all have this ability to feel the life of the Earth. When we have reawakened this sense within ourselves, we will have held our first conscious conversation with Mother Earth.

Feeling the Earth with Birds

The next time you enter a forest, open yourself to the sights and sounds made by the forest. Don't use your ears, but use your hearing. Don't use your eyes, but use your vision. If you strain to hear the sounds and see the sights, you are putting on a filter of your own preconceptions of what a forest is supposed to be like. Just open yourself up and feel nature as it really is.

Listen to the sound of a bird chirping. This sound is vibration. However, depending on how awake your inner senses are, you will register this sound merely as a chirp, ... or as a vibration of life immersed deep within your own being, through which you can feel the beating of your own heart, variations in body temperature, and the flow of blood through your veins. The sound of the bird chirping contains infinite life. Through it, you can feel the sparkling of sunlight as it strikes the bird's feathers.

You can feel the whisper of leaves on the branch that the bird is perched upon. Through the simple sound of a bird singing, you can hold a conversation with the earth.

This world is filled with the fantastic and the wonderful. However, we have considered ourselves merely an audience of such wonder, instead of being a part of it. We have limited our own sense of wonder by the narrow window of our five material senses. When we make ourselves wide open, the bird will no longer look like just a bird, but will look like the sun, moon and, most importantly, the Earth. With expanded senses, we can see the reality of ourselves as an integral part of the relationships in life, erasing the artificial barriers that our own limited thinking has created. We are all interconnected with the life that is Earth. When our senses are really open, even a rock underneath our feet is precious and a dry leaf falling from a tree in autumn, exquisite.

Earth Whispers

Earth whispers with a voice, gentle and soft

Land is my bosom
Sea is my soul
Wind is my breath
Sky is my heart
And you are all my children

Earth whispers in a voice filled with longing
Feel the sun tingling on your skin
Hear the whispers of the moon and stars
Hear the radiant symphony of nature
Speaking with one voice
Let Mago's dream come true

Feeling the Earth's Energy

Everything is energy. The earth's atmosphere is filled with energy. The land is streaming with energy. The sea is swimming with energy. The hills and the mountains are spewing out energy every second. The reality of every entity and object is energy. Through the sensation of 'Ki' energy, we can feel the Earth's body. Raise your hands into the air. What do you feel? You will feel air passing through your fingers. Earth's breath is hidden in the stream of air that passes through your fingers. Rotate your hands and feel how the wind, the breath changes.

Now place your hands in front of your chest, palms facing each other. Focus your attention on your palms, and concentrate on the subtle but definite sensation in your palms. First, you will feel heat, but then, you will start to feel the beating of your own pulse within the heat. Concentrate on the pulse, allowing its rhythm to ring throughout your being. Now, bring your hands closer to each other, without touching, and then slowly pull them apart. Concentrate on your palms. You may feel anything from a prolonged sense of deep warmth to a subtle tingling or tickling sensation. Now, imagine that there is a small ball that you are holding. Cup your hands and rotate them along the contours of the ball. Feel the balloon-like presence of the energy within your hands, soft yet firm, amorphous yet shapely, in constant flux within your hands.

What you are feeling is 'Ki,' energy of Mago, the Earth. Immerse your consciousness in this sea of energy, feeling it expand along your arms, your shoulders, your face, and downward, as if a soft, warm rain is soothing every part of your body. You feel the breath of Mago, and her love. Our soul is riding upon this stream of energy to become one and to commune with Mago, the soul of the Earth. This energy is peace, absolute freedom, allowing you to break out of the shell that is your body. You can now send this stream of energy to your loved ones, using it to comfort and heal. In merging with Mago's energy, we can soothe our hearts, harmonize the flow of energy within our body and mind, and replenish our bodies' vitality.

Let us try to feel Mago's energy through our breath. Open your hearts and minds. Breathe in and out while concentrating on your Dahnjon, a point in your lower abdomen, two inches below your navel. With a straight back, focus all your attention on that one area, letting go of all thoughts. Concentrate and breathe. Through your breath, you are going beyond the realm of time and space. You are entering into the world of nothingness, the beginning and end of all life. Breathe in deeply, and breathe out. Concentrate on your breath only, for nothing else exists. Eliminate any thoughts through your breath. You will feel the energy of Mago in your breathing, for as you breathe, she breathes, creating a rhythm of life that has always nurtured you. It is a rhythm that you haven't yet consciously recognized. Let this rhythm of life flow to the ends of your limbs and throughout your body and you will experience a 'knowing'. This is not an intellectual exercise, but an experiential one, of knowing the Earth through your heart. Now you have spoken your first words to Mother Earth, Mago. This is the purest phenomenon of life.

Keeping your focus on your lower Dahnjon, breathe in with the silent sound, 'Ma.' Then breathe out slowly, with the silent sound, 'go.' 'Ma-go...' 'Ma-go...' Let these silent words echo in your Dahnjon, in your mind and in the chambers of your heart, until they come alive and drive your breath.

Mago, Mother Earth, is even now sending her life-giving breath to us with every breath we take, accompanied by her plea for Mago's Dream. When you feel an empty tiredness in your heart, wanting warmth and energy, join in the breathing of Mago. You will always be welcome.

Feeling the Earth's Heart

We can most immediately and closely recognize the inner heart and love of Mother Earth through the maternal love of our own mothers, for these two loves spring from the same source. To save a sick child, a mother would gladly donate one of her kidneys without a second thought. No, she would probably even donate her only heart to save a dying child. Such is the amazing power of maternal love. When faced with the threat of danger to her child, her maternal love turns a mother into a powerful and protective force of nature. When you expand the love of a mother to include all life on Earth, you have glimpsed the love of Mago.

Maternal love is not learned. Maternal love is not created through religious ritual or faith. Maternal love is part of our human heritage, received from the mother of our mothers. If we travel upstream to the source of this river of love, there we will find the love of Mago, Mother Earth, pouring forth. We are all born into this stream of love, ageless and endless. Within the comforting bosom of your own mother lies the deeper love of Mago. When we all realize this, the eyes of our divinity will open.

Close your eyes and call forth the name of love in your hearts, 'Ma-go...' 'Mago'...

As you repeatedly call out her name, you will find yourself speaking the name of your mother or the sound of 'Mother'... 'Mom'... as you had when you were child and thought you had lost her in some crowded mall or street. No one was born without a mother. Not even Jesus. Just as our own mothers have nurtured us, so has Mother Earth nurtured humanity as a whole, without regard to race, religion or nation.

Feel the love of Mother Earth soothe your heart, filling and honoring it. And let the peaceful silence gently envelop you with comfort and serenity.

Becoming One with the Earth's Soul, Mago

Physical bodies cannot truly join together to become one. However, souls can become a unified and true One. If you know 'Ki' energy, your soul can merge into wholeness, for energy forms the bridge upon which souls travel.

Bring your hands together in front of your chest, palms facing each other. Once again, feel the energy between your palms, eyes lightly closed and concentrating on your hands. Imagine your right hand as your soul and the left, the soul of the Earth, Mago. Feel the energy form a bridge between your hands, connecting them and allowing them to commune. Feel the bridge of energy draw your hands nearer to each other, bringing your soul closer to the soul of the Earth, merging with the life of Mago. Your hands have come together. And you have met the soul of the Earth. You have experienced Mago.

Mother Earth
Remember me
I am seeking you
To complete my soul

Mother Earth
Remember me
Allow my soul
Into your Oneness

My dream as your dream
My dream as Mago's dream
Mago's dream as my reason
For coming here to the Earth

Mother Earth
Remember me
I seek to fulfill Mago's dream

For Earth's everlasting peace.

Let the envelope of energy sheath you in its' comforting warmth. Let yourself go with the current of this sea of energy, swaying gently to and fro, side to side, searching for balance and harmony of motion. Let your hands unfurl in front of you and move according to the dictates of the energy flow. This is the energy dance, or the dance of three persons. The three persons are you, Mago, and the two that have merged into One. Your hands float and move alongside your swaying head, all separately with individual expression, to a unifying, underlying rhythm. When you lose yourself, as defined by your ego, you will find a bigger and more powerful you, residing within the matrix of energy, that links and unifies all souls. Move, as you will, as Mago will. Cry, as you will, as you feel Mago cry. Love, as you will, as Mago has shown. Heal, as you will, as Mago is healing. Live, as you will, as Mago has allowed.

By feeling the love, pain, and life of Mago that she herself feels and expresses through the nurturing of everything on Earth, you will indeed have become the Mother Earth herself. You will have felt the pain of Mago when

3,000 innocent lives were lost in the World Trade Towers. You will have felt the grief of Mago when babies starve to death in inhumane conditions, not because of the parsimony of land, but because of the blind cruelty of local warlords and governments. You will also have felt the singing joy of love when the echo of a kind, unselfish act travels around the world on a current of good will. You will have felt these as Mago. Use these insights to spur you along on your journey to the perfection of your soul, for that is ultimately the reason that we have been born to this Earth. Physical bodies will perish, but your soul will have traveled that much farther to its destination.

Ode to Mother Earth

At the moment of union with the soul of Mother Earth, you will feel complete peace and perfect love. And you will be connected to the soul of humanity, for the Earth loves all of humanity fairly and equally. The Earth doesn't use spoken or written language. If she had to speak to us using the medium of language, her words would be imperfect and incomplete, for no language can be perfect and complete. The Earth herself is complete unto herself. The

Earth herself is a perfect language, with no further adjectives or adverbs needed. The Earth herself is the common language that can bind all of humanity into a unified web of Oneness.

Love and peace are not transmitted through words, but through the soft light of the eyes and curved lips of a gentle smile. Loved ones feel each other's love without need for words. We can find the smile of Mago in the flight of a bird and the crashing of waves. We can feel the love of Mago in her bounty, and in the comfort of her rain. Such is the language of the Earth, communicated through the energy of the soul. Such is Cosmic Energy (Chunjikiun) and Cosmic Mind (Chunjimaeum). If we can feel the love of Mother Earth and embrace the whole world and humanity with such love, then this is Truth. There is no higher truth, ... no deeper enlightenment. When you feel this love, not just with your brain but with your heart, shaking you to the core of your being with its warmth and power, then you will be able to communicate this love to others. You will have become a healer of yourself and the Earth.

Mother Earth, Mago
I have realized today
That I am, an Earth-Human
Precious part of life's grandeur
Existing on Earth
Belonging to Earth
Nurtured by Earth
Fed by the Earth
Sleeping on Earth
Feeling... the Earth
In my bones, and blood
As I breathe with Earth

Mother Earth, Mago
I have realized today
I shall return to the Earth someday
For my body is yours
My sleeping is yours
My everything... is yours
Nothing that is mine is truly mine
But borrowed
During my time on Earth
My loved ones

Are also Earth-Humans

All feared ones

Of every race, religion, and nation

Are also Earth-Humans

Family that shares the same bed

Eats from the same table

Demanding respect

Forged from family ties

Ties that bind us... to all life on Earth

For peace on Earth

For peace within myself

For peace I shall live

Earth-Humans and Mago's Three Great Truths

I was born in a very small country town near the city of ChunAhn in Central, South Korea. Whenever I think of my hometown, the first thing that comes to my mind is the sound of cicadas chirping noisily, and nearby streams gurgling softly. These sounds are intermixed with the familiarity of memories, of the setting sun sinking behind the nearby hills, and of a parade of the familiar faces of my parents and neighbors. These create a warm, cozy feeling of home. Memories of my hometown are very precious to me, as I am sure they are to you.

Hometown to most of us is more than just a place, a

stretch of land marked off on an impersonal map. Home is at the very core of our lives, regardless of whether our memories of home are happy or not. Whenever we think of home, we feel a certain wistfulness and seek to preserve its' memories, pure and unsullied. When we see our hometown changed into the latest version of a cookie cutter development, filled with concrete convenience and automation in the name of modernity and economic prosperity, we feel a certain sense of loss at the lack of the original spirit of home. We unconsciously wonder if there was something more we could have done to keep our home pristine and intact. It would be complicated to try to explain the extent of the psychological and emotional investment that we have in the concept of home.

However, it is clear that we feel we have a great stake in, and kinship with our home, precisely because it is 'our' home, not yours or theirs. We have a sense of identity and a feeling of connectedness to others, that comes from sharing a common home.

I live in a place called Earth.

So do you.

We are Earth-Humans.

Say the following to yourselves out loud: "I am an

Earth-Human." Do you like the sound of it? It might sound awkward at first, but soon you will realize how true it is and wonder why it sounded awkward in the first place. Did you ever feel awkward when you said to yourself, "I am an American"? No, you probably felt a conscious or an unconscious sense of pride about being an American. Rightfully so. Then why should it sound awkward, and why shouldn't you feel the same sense of pride when you tell yourself that you are an 'Earth-Human?' Say it again, out loud. Now feel the meaning of the words. When you think of the Earth, do you think of it as your home? Is your awareness deep, or large enough to accept the reality of the Earth as your home? If so, do you feel up to accepting the love, pride, and responsibility that you hold for your home, the Earth?

What Does Loving the Earth Mean?

Many people claim to love the Earth. However, what does that mean? Just as loving home does not refer to just caring for the land and the house, loving the Earth cannot refer to just environmental protection. Loving the Earth must mean that one acknowledges the Earth as one, unified community. We must protect our home as part of a family and contribute our all, as does the citizen of a country, deriving a sense of pleasure and accomplishment from this. This is what loving the Earth should mean.

An Earth-Human is someone who is in touch with the body, mind, and energy of the Earth. An Earth-Human acknowledges the Earth as the ultimate arbitrator of 'living values' and applies such values to his or her everyday life. An Earth-Human knows that 'Earth and I are One', ultimately leading to Oneness of the whole of humanity. An Earth-Human therefore cares for and heals his or her neighbors and family members as his or her own body, with the all encompassing, non-discriminating love of Mago. An Earth-Human is a healer in every sense of the word.

When our awareness has made that leap and joined with Earth's awareness, we will have gained the strength and wisdom to overcome our insignificant boundaries of self and group-egotism, and be able to feel love for all life on Earth.

Some people argue that we should not limit our awareness to the Earth in this age of space travel and space stations. What they do not realize is that being truly aware of the Earth will allow us to attain an awareness of the cosmos as well, for they are intimately interrelated. In fact, they are one and the same. The moment you become aware of the Earth, you will be awakened to cosmic awareness. You will have had to unbind the chains of all preconceptions and self-defeating ideas of limitation in order to develop a point of view that includes the whole Earth. This can only be done with cosmic awareness.

Looking at the whole of the universe, the Earth is tinier than the tiniest speck of dust in the room of the cosmos. However, collective human consciousness has not evolved far enough to even grasp the wholeness of the Earth. To talk about cosmic awareness while we are struggling to accept the Oneness of the Earth, our home, is premature.

Furthermore, if we make an effort to engage in conscious evolution of our awareness, we will realize that we are One with the cosmos, at the very moment we realize we are One with the Earth. Earth simply provides us with a more concrete target for the path of our consciousness evolution. Perhaps, you could call it a sneaky path to enlightenment paved with only the best intentions.

Just as Earth is the tiniest of the tiniest part of the universe, humanity is only a small segment of life that populates her, despite our illusions of grandeur. A human being can elevate his or her consciousness enough to feel the entirety of the Earth in his or her heart, and to realize the Oneness that connects all of life in a web of live, pulsating energy.

That human being will then look at the Earth and all life as 'home,' and with the love and protectiveness that home generates. Such is the amazing power of awareness transformation. Such is the amazing result of enlightenment. And the far more amazing thing is that we, as human beings, have been blessed with such enlightenment from birth. It is our choice to become aware of the cosmic vastness of our own consciousness, or not.

The following should be the first words spoken to a newborn: "Welcome to the Earth. You are now an Earth-Human, whose life roots are buried deep inside the heart of the Earth." This should the very first thing that a baby learns. This should be the first message that the human brain receives. This is the highest enlightenment there is; to know that you have come to Earth and that you are now an Earth-Human.

Despite the obviousness of this, people do not realize

that they have come to Earth and that Earth is the foundation of life. Nations, religions, and all else exist because of the Earth. Even space travel exists because of the Earth. However, there is no school that teaches this. There is no curriculum that expounds on the relationship between Earth and humanity. If we were to realize the true meaning of Earth and Earth-Humans, then it would be impossible to hate each other as we do today.

We did not come to the Earth to compete against one another as separate entities. We came to the Earth to found a peaceful global community centered on Earth, as a cosmic exercise in the evolution of our awareness and the growth of our souls. Only we can institute world peace. Not the moon, the stars, or even the sun. Only we, the Earth-Humans, whose awareness has expanded enough to see the reality of the Earth and earth's community of interwoven life, are capable of creating lasting peace on Earth. An Earth-Human can go beyond the boundaries of nation and religion, because his expanded consciousness recognizes the fleeting nature of artificial separation that imprisons us. We will no longer belong to one particular people, country, or religion. We will belong to the Earth, and her all-enveloping wholeness.

For an Earth-Human, the standards by which he or she lives will be determined by conscience that arises out of awareness that the Earth is at the root of all. An Earth-Human will gladly take responsibility for the future of the Earth, for an expanded awareness demands nothing less. To become an Earth-Human is to realize your spiritual heritage of enlightenment.

Mago's 1st Truth - Soul, Brain, and Brain Respiration

In midst of the horror and confusion that last year's terrorist attacks generated, I got to thinking a lot about the soul. From every corner of the world, I heard vitriolic diatribes against terrorists, calling them soulless devils. Soulless, are they? Although the loss of innocent lives cannot be excused by any means, were the terrorists really soulless? Or were they poor souls who were controlled by bad 'knowledge' or 'information' in their brains?

I wish that this world could actually be cleanly divided into good and evil, angels and devils. This way, all we would have to do is to vanquish the forces of evil once and for all. It would surely take sacrifice and courage, but once accomplished, it would be finished for all time. The world would be clean cut, and there would be no more of this confounding confusion about different points of view, justifications, and age-old cultural differences. The world would be black and white without any gray areas.

Let's say you have in front of you, the worst terrorist in the history of humankind, perhaps even Bin Laden himself. Say he is sleeping, with a face that is almost angelic, without a trace of evil. At this moment, can you call him the devil? Or is he good? Can you apply any value judgment to this person at this moment? He is neither devil nor angel. He is just a person sleeping. While sleeping, the various forms of information in his head: knowledge, intellect, will, ambition, personality, etc., are dormant in his brain and thereby powerless to influence his surroundings. It is the information inside a brain that makes a person into the devil or an angel. Depending on the information and the source of information that a person chooses to accept, he or she may stand on the side of God or Satan.

I'm sure that terrorists have parents, brothers and sisters. I'm sure that terrorists have wives or husbands or girlfriends or boyfriends who love them. And I am also sure that each one of the terrorists was the light of someone's life. The terrorists gave their lives willingly because they held a piece of information, or belief in this case, that was stronger than their instinctive hold on their very lives. They probably thought of themselves as great martyrs up to, and beyond, the moment of their own death. And were without any sense of guilt, because this information represented the overriding value in their lives. A person thus polluted by bad information not only disgraces himself but also disgraces his god, for he always justifies his actions by his faith or belief. Unfortunately, God is help-less against being painted by this same terrorist stroke because God cannot appear in court to defend himself.

The motivation of a terrorist comes from information that caters to satisfying the collective ego of the particular group to which the terrorist belongs. In order to satisfy the collective ego of the group, an individual will commit ter-rible acts of violence. His or her brain has been injected by information that not only justifies such actions in the name of country, god, tradition, history, etc., but also glo-rifies them.

The group reserves the highest places of honor for the heroes who have advanced the cause of their egotism. Therefore, the reality behind any action is the information that drives it. Bin Laden may die, but the information that defines him will not. After his death, the information will just transfer to a different host, and continue its destructive work. What does this tell us about the nature of human beings?

The value of a human being depends on the quality of information held in his or her brain. Depending on whether that information is positive or negative, destructive or constructive, loving or hateful, the direction and destiny of the person's life will be determined. However, the most important point, that we must never forget, is that no piece of information is more important than the soul. Even the gods and religions that make up our faith traditions are merely information that has been received into our brains from birth. That information did not create our souls.

It is we ourselves who are the manufacturers and distributors of information. If information acts the part of the master, there is something wrong. If information claims a place of absolute authority, not giving us the freedom of choice, then our soul will have fallen from grace. No information, however authoritative or honorable, is more important than the soul. Only one who has been awakened to the feeling of the soul within his or her heart can proclaim this with confidence. Information is manufactured. A soul cannot be manufactured.

Our soul is complete and perfect unto itself, for the Creator has created our soul. Our souls are, therefore, more precious than any information. We must always be on guard to know if our souls have been polluted by information that claims to have higher authority than the Creator. Unfortunately, today, much destructive, self-justifying information is being fabricated and is polluting our souls. Do not let any information rule your soul.

History will record this year as the year in which the World Trade Towers fell. History will know this year as the Year of September 11th. History will witness the massive grief and shock that we all felt when we first heard the news with a general sense of incredulity and foreboding. And history will surely judge us by our actions in response to such brutal acts.

I join with the rest of America and the world in praying for the souls of the departed and their families. As I spend the majority of my time in the United States, I feel unbounded love for the often-breathtaking beauty of the land, and the everlasting warmth of her people. I was personally shaken by this tragedy. This is indeed a time of grief and reflection, not only for a nation, but also for all of humanity. The attacks were horrifying to us not only because of the magnitude of destruction they wrought, not because they occurred in our backyard, and not because they threatened security in our very homes. Ultimately it was because of our inability to understand the depth of hatred that lay behind these actions. There is a wall of 'unknowability' of the sheer rage exhibited by such actions. What could drive human beings, to purposely sacrifice their own lives to kill and maim thousands of innocent others in order to make a point?

When I look at the horrific aftermath of the attacks, I ask: "What point could possibly have been so important to cause such bloodshed?" "What cause could possibly have been so crucial to cause bodies and limbs to rain down on the streets of New York City?" "What national or international interest can be so paramount that innocent babies must be riddled with nails from a crude bomb, or a child be shot and bleed to death next to his father?"

We feel anger, rage, and an urge to retaliate against the perpetrators of these dastardly deeds. We want justice served, which often means inflicting the same or greater amount of pain on the parties responsible for these acts.

However, when the emotions of the moment pass, and they do pass, and we have performed these 'acts of justice,' we are often left with an empty feeling of loss and sadness. And ultimately we are left asking: "Why do these things continue to happen?"

It is because individuals have allowed information to become paramount to their own souls. They have let their guard down.

The question we are left with is, "How do we make sure that this never happens again?" Can it be through retribution? Perhaps that will provide a respite in the short run, but ultimately, it will create more 'martyrs-to-be' than peace. No, the cause of all conflict is information. The only way to stop this cycle of violence is to erase bad information and to replace it with good information. What is good information then? It is information that will allow your soul to grow, information that will allow our consciousness to evolve to a higher level and information that will contribute to the betterment of the world's people and the Earth. This is the most fundamental way to heal society.

Humans are the manufacturers and distributors of information. We are the owners and consumers of information. We have the right to repair any malfunctioning information, and to throw any unusable information onto the garbage heap. Only good information can repair bad information. Information can only be changed by information.

Now that we know what the prescription is, how do we take it? We take it through the brain. Our brain is the system into which information enters to be processed and stored. We utilize the information in our brains to develop a system of living called civilization. Therefore, understanding the brain is analogous to understanding humans, and consequently the civilization that has been wrought by humans.

Everyone has a brain. However, not many of us live our lives as masters of our own brains. Most of us allow others to run our brains for us, with information that they have manufactured and promoted. From the moment of our birth, our brain has been subject to information that has been fabricated by others. This began with our parents and their preconceptions of the world, which then became our preconceptions. In school, our brains became the domain of the teachers; in church, our brains became the domain of the preachers; in temples our brains were the domain of bonzes or rabbis. Unless you have a certain protective filter with which to judge information that comes into your brain, and are able to compare it to standards that you have set for yourself, it soon becomes very difficult to assess which information is good for you. Thus you allow external information to control the workings of your brain.

The master of our brain is our soul. Not anything or anyone else. However, many masters are asleep in the bedroom upstairs while uninvited guests are acting the part of master downstairs. Our brain is run by information generated by specific nations, religions, ethnic groups, and other groups whose goals are perhaps not the same as ours. Our brains are being ruled by information that is promoted by others.

How long are you going to let this go on? You haven't signed a legally binding lease with any of these people or groups. You can recover your brain as soon as you decide to. Don't let your brain be a slave to information manufactured by others and distributed under such brand names as tradition, religion, politics, philosophy and so forth. Our brains are to be used by us, and only by us, to facilitate the growth of our souls. Our brains must not be used to advance the cause or agenda of any particular group, no matter how noble their stated goals may be.

The first step in taking back your own brain is to realize that you and your soul are the true masters of your brain. Even information disguised in the prettiest costumes, tempting you with sweet-sounding promises of security, wealth, or fame, cannot truly be the master of your brain.

The second step is to set a standard for yourself by which you can judge whether a piece of information is good for you or not. What is this yardstick that you can use to judge the value of a piece of information? It is the Earth. If you measure all information by whether or not it has constructive value for the betterment of Earth, then you can easily tell the true nature of the information and its' origin. Any information that seeks to lead you to advance the agenda of a particular group at the expense of others, and to justify such actions with sweet sounding logic, is not information that will help your soul mature.

Understanding that good information is our medicine, how shall we take it? We know that vitamins are good for us so we take them in a tablet or pill with some orange juice. For our purposes, there are many medicines in the world which contain similar ingredients and that will work well. The one I am prescribing is called Brain Respiration. Brain Respiration is a way to facilitate intake of the medicine. The medicine is 'good information,' and Brain Respiration is the needle and the syringe with which to inject the good medicine.

Brain Respiration utilizes Ki-energy to help you become the master of your own brain. Ki-energy, although invisible and silent, is a form of communication. You can use Ki-energy not only to communicate with others but also to clear your brain of the negativity you must encounter everyday. Brain Respiration is, in short, a method of processing the information in your brain, organizing the files, determining the most recent and most often used documents, judging the value of each document to the task at hand, and deleting or reorganizing the files for greater efficiency.

Now, lift your hands in front of your chest, with your hands about two inches apart. Imagine a ball of Ki-energy in front of your heart, lightly cupping it with your hands. Concentrate on the ball, with complete attention. Notice a sensation of heat, electricity, or a feeling of tingling current. Let these flow over your hands and into your arms, traveling upward into your shoulders and neck. Slowly move your hands, bringing them closer together and then pulling them apart. Together and apart, and feel the sensation of energy become stronger with each repetition. Holding on to this feeling of energy, bring your right hand up to the right side of your brain. Move your hand all around the right side of your head in a soothing and massaging motion, with about four inches of space in between your hand and your head. Imagine, and actually feel, the stream of energy generated by your hand as it enters the right side of your head and massages your brain, allowing it to relax. Now repeat the process for the left side of your head.

Now that your brain is relaxed, breathe out with a powerful whoosh... and imagine all the negativity and bad information being expelled from your body through your breath. Information is transmitted and communicated through waves of energy. Conversely, you can expel all of the negative information through waves of energy that you have created, releasing it through your breath. And not only through your nose and mouth, but also through your ears and eyes, and through every single pore of your skin. Feel the negativity being expelled and excreted by the power of your own energy.

Next feel yourself creating a refreshing current of clean, pure energy, relaxing and comforting you as it fills your whole being. Now feel your brain again and say to yourself, "I am the master of my own brain." Have a conversation with your brain. How many of us have lived our lives without conscious awareness of our brain, not realizing that it is our brain that determines the path of our lives and the destiny of our souls?

The two most important kinds of information in this world today are about the brain and the Earth. Not merely geological information about the Earth, but about how we can make the Earth the ultimate, and purely objective and loving judge of our values and information. And not just anatomical information about the brain, but about how we can become masters of our brains and use them for the growth of our souls, both individually, and collectively as humanity.

Change the brain, and change the world. Change your world and our world. Take back your brain from the clutches of manufacturers of information with their myriad of agendas that have sown confusion in the world. Fill your brain with information that will bring about peace in our world. Fill your brain with information that will work for the betterment of all. Do this, and you will be participating in a revolutionary movement of souls that will encompass the world.

Mago's 2nd Truth - A Free Soul

The greatest blessing in being human is that we have a soul. And we have a way to perfect and complete the journey of our soul, for this is what we came to the Earth to do. All enlightened masters and saints have said this same thing.

If you were to ask me what a 'completed' or 'perfected' soul is, I would say it is a soul that feels peace through its entirety. And for that to happen, a soul must become One with the soul of the Earth through a process of communication and communion. A soul that has experienced communion with the soul of the Earth will have seen and experienced the Oneness that can never be separated or divided. This will facilitate understanding of the reality that connects all of our souls into One. A person who has not realized Oneness is bound to be lonely and anxious, chasing after temporary highs of wealth and fame that are never truly satisfying, for these cannot fill the emptiness that the soul feels.

We turn to religions and faith traditions to fill the emptiness that comes from ignorance of the soul's Oneness. However, any peace or fulfillment that we derive from such practices is also bound to be temporary and fleeting, unless these practices include communion with the soul of the Earth. Not as you would communicate with a god of a religion, but as a fundamental realization of Oneness, of the 'Bigness' of the Earth that encompasses every nation, religion, and people.

The Earth is not a private club; it is a universal club. Being born allows you to receive a membership card; you don't have to do anything else for it. And it is the most beautiful club that you will ever find. Once you have realized that you are a member, don't you want to keep it clean and comfortable for fellow members to use? And once you realize that you are a member, will you allow bickering or fighting among the members over silly things like dress code or the food that's being served? And as a member, will you stand by, letting only certain members hog all the food or reserve all the tee times in advance without regard to other members' needs? As a member, will you hoodwink the new members out of their rightful privileges as full members, hiding and co-opting their privileges for your own, or stand by while others do? Of course not.

Only by recognition of our Earth membership can we achieve a true and equitable peace. And for this realization to occur, in the most fundamental and unforgettable way, our souls need to become One with the soul of the Earth. First, we first need to free our soul of its burdens and set it free. A free soul... how do we achieve this? Many people pray for a free soul, filled with sincerity and earnestness. If we could achieve this through prayer alone, how easy it would all be. Humanity has been praying for thousands of years. We have prayed for freedom of the soul and for peace. We should now know that prayers alone are not enough.

To set our souls free, we first need to know the reality of a soul. Ask yourself whether you can feel your soul. When asked this question, people answer in a variety of ways: "I am deeply touched by beautiful music, ... isn't that my soul speaking to me?" "I felt a current of electricity course through me while watching the sunset over Sedona mountain ... I felt my soul at that moment." "I am deeply in love with someone right now, ... isn't that evidence of my soul?" And so on...

People tend to confuse a new sensation or their emotions with their soul. But a soul is neither an emotion nor sensation. To use an analogy, a soul is like a bowl made of clear glass. Yet it has no weight. The weight of a soul is zero. Inside this bowl of the soul, you put in many pieces of information including emotions, memories, greed, ambition, and what have you. Good and bad memories are jumbled together inside this bowl of the soul. Your painful and your precious moments are also in this bowl. People usually say that you feel your soul when you feel love and not when you feel hatred. However, both love and hatred are merely emotions. They themselves are not the soul. In fact, both to love and to hate something act as a chain that binds the soul. They are both attachments, and a free soul cannot be bound by attachments of any kind, however tempting and reassuring.

The weight of a soul is zero. Only zero is pure and without attachments. Only zero is free. Only at this point of zero, can we make a new choice. To a soul at the point of zero, concepts such as freedom and salvation are just pieces of information, nothing more or less. A free soul, in a state of zero, is itself enlightenment and salvation and heaven. A free soul is the state of emptiness and nothingness. We can make a truly new choice in such a state. If we have something in our hands, then we can't grab a hold of anything else. If our proverbial cup isn't empty, we can't pour something into it. Only in this state of zero, will our soul be free to create anew, and to join with the soul of the Earth. Always try to maintain this state of zero. Use fame, money, and success as tools, but never become attached to them, for attachments will enslave you.

A free soul can truly be at rest. Only a free soul can see the world clearly, seeing form as it is, superficial and fleeting. A free soul, in the state of zero, is like a scale that you can use to weigh everything around you. But be sure to remove the things you have measured, so that the scale of the soul can go back to zero. Returning to zero does not mean that everything disappears and nothing remains. Your experience remains. If you are wise, you will use this experience to fertilize and nurture your soul. In addition to self-confidence and respect for others, you will have gained an indescribably deep sense of inner peace. This is the true meaning of maturity of the soul.

In kindergarten we learned to put a toy back in its

place once we were finished playing with it. What a child gets out of playing with a toy is not the toy itself, nor the temporary emotional delight, but the maturity he or she gains from the experience. If the child seems too attached to the toy and refuses to let go of it, we recognize it as a worrisome sign of possible emotional or mental disturbance. Humanity is currently too attached to the toy, and not to the lesson that playing may impart, to further the maturity of our collective soul.

Only a free soul can see the Truth. Our brain has the power to set our souls free. Become the master of your brain and the liberator of your soul.

Lift up your right hand, palm facing up in a cupped shape. Imagine the glass bowl of your soul resting on top of your right hand. Inside this bowl lie all your attachments and emotions, your loves and hates, your precious moments and the painful ones, pride and embarrassment, your loved ones and your enemies. Many people seek to keep the good memories and throw away the bad ones. However, to have a truly free soul, you need to throw away the good as well as the bad. This is because at the moment of becoming attached to the good, the possibility of bad is created. If you love, you worry that you might get hurt. If you acquire something that pleases you, you worry that you might lose it. Both love and hatred are attachments, chains that bind the soul. This is why emptying your vessel of the soul requires wisdom and courage.

Now, slowly turn your hand over and spill out the contents. One, two, three! Turn it over and watch it all spill out. Free your soul! Watch all your attachments spill onto the ground like individual grains of sand. Empty the bowl completely. And free your soul.

Sun is light, thunder is sound, and wind is vibration.
Light, sound, and vibration are the reality behind all
    existence.
Wade upstream to the source of humanity
And you shall find light.

Light is the beginning of our life.
Movement of light created sound.
And movement of sound created vibration.
Our life is light, sound and vibration.
Without time or space.
When everything begins
And where we must return.

Our soul is light, sound, and vibration.
Trapped behind the cage of body
Hidden under the cover of emotions
And imprisoned behind bars of thought
Its light feeble and unseen
Waiting for escape and freedom.

What is enlightenment?
If not recovering the original light.
Light of life, light of the soul
What we call mysterious and fantastic
Refers to self
Our own root and source
Which we have forgotten
Leading to loneliness and despair
Loss of the soul,

A battle of souls
All lonely and lost
Wearing armor of religions
Wielding swords of ideologies
Shooting arrows of prejudice
Slaves, one and all

Ignorant of enlightenment that will set us free

Only a free soul can continue the path
Only a free soul will finish the journey
Growth of soul can be achieved through good deeds
Perfection of soul can only be attained with enlight-
  enment
Becoming one with the Earth
That is the key to perfection of the soul
Whose secret you possess already
In your brain.

Mago's 3rd Truth -
Enlightenment and the Earth-Human

Do you seek enlightenment? Why? What is the reason and
purpose for your pursuit of enlightenment?

I have known many people with romantic ideas about
enlightenment. Many people pursue enlightenment as a
means of escape, chasing after dreams of eternal peace or
freedom, or trying to escape from some real world suffering or difficulties that they feel unable to deal with.
However, this concept of enlightenment is so worthless

that you won't even get a piece of stale bread with it! Such is not enlightenment. Enlightenment is something with a definite purpose and goal. We seek enlightenment so that we may become stronger and brighter. We seek enlightenment because we seek to benefit our immediate surroundings and the world.

If you really desire enlightenment, then throw away any false romantic ideas about it. If you are seeking to surround yourself with a nebulous cloud of 'feel-good' love and peace, then you harbor a huge misconception. People often think that enlightenment is an eternal state of peace and quiet. Maybe, but you must not remain there for long if you want to continue living and creating. A child may be pure and innocent, but what power does a child have to change the direction in which an adult is walking?

Remaining in a state of peace and quiet may be good for an individual, but it is useless in bringing peace to the world. What good is an enlightened person who has no positive influence on those around him? True enlightenment imparts wisdom and the strength to make good choices in the real world. If enlightenment has no bearing on the state of the real world, what good is it? As I said, it won't buy you a piece of stale bread.

By the above definition, enlightenment is a state of mind that allows you to act for the benefit of all. In short, enlightenment can be represented by good deeds. How do you determine what good is? You already know! You already know what is good for you and your neighbors and the world. You don't need someone else to tell you what is ultimately good for humanity and the Earth. You already have an internally calibrated scale that can distinguish what is good from what is bad. Enlightenment is, therefore, an already existing state of your mind.

Therefore, enlightenment does not require effort. If you seek enlightenment through some type of effort, then it is not true enlightenment. Effort is needed to make something that is incomplete, complete. Something that is imperfect into something perfect. However, enlightenment is already perfect and complete, thereby not needing any effort at improvement.

The reason we cannot act for the benefit of all is not due to a lack of enlightenment, but because of the various prejudices, egos, and attachments that force us to cater to the needs of particular individuals or groups. When you can divest your consciousness of these influences, your consciousness by itself is complete and perfect. The realization of this is enlightenment.

Thus, enlightenment is not something that you have to strive for; it is something felt and realized naturally. This is why your enlightenment and my enlightenment, your truth and my truth are not different from one another. Because truth is unchanging, it can be communicated and transmitted to others and expressed in actions. If enlightenment cannot be communicated and truth cannot be shared among all, then such things are merely personal illusions of grandeur.

Until now, we have had the wrong idea about the role of religion. We thought that religion would help human beings receive salvation and achieve enlightenment. Under this premise, religions have exercised great influence over every aspect of our lives, with absolute authority, controlling our souls and imprisoning our awareness. Let us look at religion again. We have to look at the basic premise of religion. A particular religion always claims to be the best one, the only one, and the unique way to reach God and receive salvation of the soul. Applying our sense of fair play, how right can this be? That you can only go to heaven if you are a Christian? That you will only reach nirvana if you only pray to Buddha?

Religion should be understood as being just a tool with which to reach an awakening of the soul, not as something with absolute authority and ultimate value. Instead of faith practice aimed at guaranteeing that individuals will reach heaven, people should search for the kernel of truth in the teachings of the different faith traditions of the world. You don't have to belong to a particular religion to be a spiritual person.

Many of us have certain prejudices and preconceptions about saints and enlightened masters. These preconceptions create an illusion about that person. For example, suppose Buddha stepped into a bath full of water that was too hot, mistakenly prepared by one of his disciples. Do you think that the Buddha would sit in the bath, with a smile on his face anyway? Would he just sit there while his skin was being scalded because he had to be always merciful and forgiving? Or do you think that would jump out of his bath, yelling, "Ouch!" If Buddha had a normal sense of touch, then the latter would probably have been the case.

Many of us have misgivings about even thinking about Buddha in this light, because we don't want to take the veneer of sanctity and otherworldliness away from him. But is this for him or us? Buddha was a human being who went through many upon many hardships before recognizing his enlightenment. He himself taught that everyone could become a Buddha. However, many people have instead chosen to place Buddha inside a shell of illusion of our their own making, without regard to the actual message of his teachings.

Likewise, many people regard Jesus Christ as someone who can never be considered a human being, despite his having chosen to die on the cross just to prove this. If we only regard Jesus as a divine being that we humans can never approach, how can we become like him? Instead of trying to live as these Masters have, we often encase them in an altar of worship, using them to soothe our own conscience once or twice a week by begrudgingly going to a church or temple. Do you think that Jesus would have preferred us to live the life of Jesus, rather than merely worship the life of Jesus? I think so.

I have repeatedly said that enlightenment is a choice. It is the choice to acknowledge or deny the enlightenment that we already possess within. Therefore, enlightenment is not a finish line. It is just a starting point. Acknowledge the perfect and complete enlightenment within you, and realize that you are the master of your own choices and your own life. Then you will be ready to begin a life of universal, spiritual responsibility. The really important thing is not whether you consciously realize that you have joined the elite ranks of the enlightened ones, but that you make your daily choices based on what you see, hear, and feel and take responsibility for those choices.

Imagine a bell in front of us, and a stick that you use to strike the bell. Enlightenment is that you know that a bell sits front of you. However, enlightenment itself does not bring about change. The bell may sit there for the next thousand years and nary a sound will be heard if someone does not pick the stick up and strike the bell. Without someone who will act to bring the bell and the stick together, that bell will never become a true bell. It will be just a lump of metal.

Only when action follows knowledge is true creation witnessed. A state of enlightenment must be followed by action in order to have any meaning in this world. Therefore, the important thing is not enlightenment, but your choice to act.

People make the mistake of thinking that enlighten-ment will automatically lead to good choices. However, this is far from the truth. Our choices are based on our ingrained habits and patterns. Realization of enlightenment only tells us which choices are good and which are bad, but this does not necessarily guarantee that we will make good choices.

Our established behavior patterns are always trying to lead us in the same direction because they are comfortable and familiar. We make judgments and choices based on what we see, hear, and feel. Life itself can be called a continuous series of choices. Whether we realize our own innate enlightenment or not, we continue to see, hear, feel and base our judgments and our choices on these underpinnings.

Unless you have a handicap or a deficiency in your senses, there is no difference in what you see, hear, and feel from what I see, hear, and feel, regardless of whether or not you realize that you are enlightened. In other words, enlightenment does not by itself guarantee that you will make the best choices. Of course, the ability to see, hear or feel something as it is will assist you in making a wise decision. It does not necessarily lead you to make the best possible choice. Ultimately, the process of making a choice depends not on acknowledgment or realization, but on your sense of discipline and character. Your choices are based on your character.

The root of your character is in your habits. A once-in-a-blue-moon choice does not speak to your character. A countless number of choices will gel into a habit, out of which the flower of your character will bloom. Good character is a fruit borne by a tree of good habits. Your goal should not be to attain enlightenment, for enlightenment is given to you already, whether you realize it or not, admit it or not.

Enlightenment exists within you, independent of your choice. Your responsibility lies in nurturing good character, bearing the best possible fruit or the most beautiful flower, from a perfect seed in the Garden of God. Your soul is this divine seed. We call this divinity. All souls are perfect. Depending on which soil you plant this seed in and what care you give, it will bear fruit or flower of different sizes, shapes, fragrances, and flavors. The process of planting and nurturing this seed is a series of endless choices. An accumulation of such choices will become your habits, the tree from which the flower, your character, will blossom forth.

Some people use the excuse, 'Because I am not

enlightened, I cannot make the right choices.' Now we know that this is axiomatically false, for your enlightenment is already a part of your birth package. Such excuses are exactly that, excuses. We must now all become people who not only recognize our enlightenment, but who actively use it to make good choices. We must go from knowing to doing. This is an Earth-Human.

Healing is expression of an Earth-Human and of his or her commitment to actualize the enlightenment within. When enough of us open our eyes to the truth of healing, then healing will not be relegated to the scrap heap of history as just another fad. It will give birth to a world wide cultural phenomenon that will heal our society and the Earth. Healing is a gift given to those who have chosen enlightenment in their lives.

During a recent lecture someone asked me, his face hard set with doubt, "Are you really enlightened?" I answered him with a question, "Do you know what enlightenment is?" He said no. Then I told him, "If you don't know what enlightenment is, you would neither believe me if I were to tell you that I am enlightened, nor if I told you that I am, in fact, not enlightened." He pressed on, again with an expression of someone reluctantly mining for the truth, "Then, what was it that you were enlightened to?" Laughing, I answered him, "I was enlightened to the fact that there is nothing to be enlightened about."

I don't want to overemphasize enlightenment. What would I achieve by emphasizing enlightenment to those who already have it? The important thing is for us to believe in ourselves. It is for us to express that belief through our healing actions, eventually changing society and the world. This is the highest evidence of enlightenment there is. Because enlightenment is a deeply personal and abstract concept, how else would you prove your enlightenment except through healing actions?

We have come to the Earth to perfect and complete the journey of our souls. The only way to do that is by healing, in every sense of the word. To heal, we need to awaken to the reservoir of enlightenment within us, and use this enlightenment to guide us in making choices.

I believe that we need at least 100 million healers in this world within ten years. No, we need them in even less time than that. These 100 million healers will constitute a critical mass that will change the destiny of the Earth. In contrast to the acts of killing that we are witnessing everyday, we will engage in acts of healing, acting to uplift our collective human consciousness... until we realize one day, that we are indeed living in Heaven on Earth.

Healing, this is the only way to peace and the only evidence of enlightenment.

Mago's Dream

Learning to Exhale into a Spiritual Civilization

We are breathing at this moment and will do so to the end of our lives. Feel your breath, gentle and calm. Breathe in slowly, and breathe out... just as slowly. Deeply. Inhale until your lungs are filled to their capacity, full to the brim with fresh air. What then? What do you have to do next to complete your breathing cycle? Exhale, of course. In order to complete the cycle of breathing, and live, you have to exhale every time you inhale.

Breath is life. When the cycle of inhaling and exhaling ends, life ends. A new life first begins with breath.

Our lives are analogous to the process of breathing. We inhale in life, growing and maturing, and then we begin to slowly exhale, getting older, eventually returning to where we started. Beginning and end are not separate, but one. Life's indescribable beauty and sacredness arise out of this Oneness. All of life is a dance to this endless cycle of breathing.

In a day, we breathe in and out countless times. We cannot exist without this cycle of in and out. Despite our differences in race and culture, we can be sure about one thing. Human life, culture and everything else are maintained because of the existence of breath. We are One through breath, if nothing else. We breathe the same sky in through our noses, and with our mouths we eat the same fruit of the Earth. All of our lives are drawn from the same sky and the same earth. We are an artistic expression created by the joyful union of heaven and earth.

Unfortunately, we are living today without this conscious realization of our common roots. We are still endlessly repeating the mistakes of the past, carelessly disregarding and stepping on other life because of our perceived differences, and because of our ever-present fear of losing in the endless game of competition that we have made of life.

Time to Exhale Slowly

Now, let us breathe again. Breathe in deeply. Breathe in until you can't breathe in any more. Then pause. Stop. Do nothing. Do not breathe out. Remain still. I believe that we are at this exact moment as a civilization. This is the moment of the pause in breathing that marks the boundary between inhaling and exhaling. We, as humanity, and as a civilization, have inhaled to our lungs' capacity. And now it's time to breathe out. What will happen to an individual if he or she insists on breathing in without breathing out? What will happen to a civilization? What will happen to us if we insist on continuing on this path of breathing in without pausing to breathe out? Our lungs will explode, ending life, as we know it. Only when you breathe out, can you again breathe in. This is a complete cycle, a full circulation. And life is a series of cycles. Life itself is a great cycle. And nothing less than the truth is in the cycle.

We as humanity are at a transitional point in our current materialistic civilization. The driving force of our civilization has been competition. However, competition cannot satisfy everyone, for it is a system of separating people into winners and losers. For every winner there is a loser, for every success a failure, and for every feeling of happiness, a sense of despair, creating a pool of losers filled with insecurity and fear. This will eventually express itself as violence, creating even more victims who seek to vent their fear and anger through violence. In this cycle of competition, winning is necessarily temporary. Winning plants the seed of its eventual downfall by the creation of 'losers.' As time goes by, more losers are created for every winner, creating a social caste system of an elite group of winners controlling and dominating an increasingly large number of losers. This creates a correspondingly large pool of insecurity, fear, and anger. Such is the world that our materialistic civilization has created through ceaseless competition, ... a far cry from the peace and harmony that we all pay lip service to.

If we seek to prevent our civilization from running headlong into an abrupt and spectacular end, we must at least stop breathing in. Our lung capacity has been reached. In order to continue this grand cycle of life, we have to start breathing out. We can exhale quickly or slowly, but we must exhale. Only then can we begin breathing in again. We must realize the wisdom of simple breathing. A choice lies before us. Will we stop inhaling? Will we stop this self-destructive game of endless competition? Or will we explode, knowing the danger, but unable or unwilling to pause to let our breath out? Our decision will depend on our level of wisdom, courage, and ultimately, consciousness.

For the very survival of humanity, we need to collectively let our breath out. However, we cannot do it so quickly that we destroy our whole system of civilization in our haste. Let us start with simple things that require a similarly simple shift in our collective awareness. Let us begin by realizing that we are all One, and practice mutual respect for our diversity.

For someone who is holding his breath, one minute will seem like an eternity. If you tell him to breathe in more without breathing out, how will he feel? Grateful, do you think? I think not. No one can exist for long without completing this natural cycle. No one can exist without breathing out after breathing in. This law applies to whole civilizations as well as to individuals. This law of the cycle even applies to the earth and the universe. Our

breath is intricately tied to the breath of the earth. Will we hear the wonderful sound of relief as we begin to breathe out, or will we wheeze and struggle to force more air into our already filled lungs?

So we need to breathe out. We need a unified shift in the direction of our civilization. This cannot happen with just one or two persons, one or two groups, or even one or two countries. We need to breathe a world wide collective sigh of relief. Instead of an army of experts who see different parts of the picture, we need to be enlightened enough to see the whole picture. With the wisdom to complete the circle of life, we may begin again. Will we make this choice ourselves, or will the choice be forced upon us?

In the next ten years, we need one hundred million people around the world who realize the wisdom of breathing out, for the simple act of exhaling will have become the ultimate act of love for humanity and love for the Earth. We have this next ten years to begin to breathe out on our own. Otherwise, we shall have forfeited our right to breathe, period. We will have the air forcibly pumped out of our lungs by the inexorable process of life.

We need one hundred million people who will start

the process of collective exhaling. Those one hundred million people will be the salvation for all of humanity. One hundred million enlightened souls. Will you be one of the hundred million?

A Spiritual Civilization

We are in the last stages of the materialistic civilization whose ultimate goal has been the pursuit of external values. The driving forces behind our civilization have been competition and domination. In the ceaseless pursuit of better, faster, and more, we have destroyed our natural resources and found our hearts to be lonely and empty. Poverty of the heart exists in midst of material wealth. Just as the moon wanes after it is full, it is time for materialistic civilization to wane in order to make way for a new cycle of human civilization, a new cycle of life. We really have only one option before us, ... a spiritual civilization.

A spiritual civilization is not a repudiation of material abundance. It is a more mature civilization that creates harmony of the whole by restoring a healthy balance between the spiritual and the material. A spiritual civilization will share the collective goal of pursuing the material as a means to spiritual development, not of pursuing the material for its own sake. A spiritual civilization will utilize material abundance for growth of the soul, and place the earth, rather than specific religions, people, or nations, at the center of its value system. It will not pursue external success, but completion in a holistic sense. And it will be a civilization that does not force people to pursue the self-limiting values of money, fame, and power by forcibly taking them from others in competition. Rather it will assist us in the pursuit spiritual completeness and perfection of our souls through harmony and reconciliation. Such will be a spiritual civilization.

Enlightenment as Common Sense

The cry for enlightenment and salvation has been heard throughout human history. Yet what good is enlightenment or salvation if they don't bring about lasting peace, health, and happiness for the whole of humanity? This age requires a Truth that will lead to enlightenment and salvation that can be shared by all, and not be confined by the limitations of religious dogma and national boundaries. Our age demands that we think and take action for ourselves. We can no longer afford to wait for fruitless preaching of mythical wise men.

For thousands of years, humanity has espoused countless truths. However, these truths have remained dormant, underutilized and unexplored for their real world possibilities. Actualization of the truth should be our ultimate goal. For what good is truth if it cannot be communicated to others in order to bring about constructive change in society? Thus far we have been caught up a feel good fantasy about the pursuit of truth, becoming experts in linguistic obfuscation and Monday morning quarterbacking of truth instead of its master. Even if some individuals succeed in achieving a certain level of awareness that can be termed enlightenment, what good is it if it is limited to just that one individual? Should he or she be content to remain in the throes of sanctimonious self-congratulation while the world is falling apart around them? Just as truth is useless if it cannot be communicated, enlightenment is worthless if it cannot be shared with many, many others.

The only way to awaken the seed of enlightenment and truth inside the human heart is through the human brain. Through the brain the truth will be translated into action and the sharing of enlightenment. In the era of spiritual civilization, the time of mere 'god-worship' must be over, and a new time of 'god-use' must come to fruition. This must be the age in which we do not merely worship a passive god, but use god for the growth of the human spirit.

God is another name for Truth. How long shall we continue to create truths for own convenience, worship them, then continue to destroy and pillage, justifying everything in the name of God? How long shall we continue to worship the ideas of mercy, justice and charity, praying and paying lip service to their sanctity and desirability, while caging them in a prison of religious and ideological dogma, never taking them out to use? Let us now use mercy. Let us now show clemency. Let us now demonstrate justice. There will never be peace without justice, nor will there be harmony without mercy and charity. This era must be an era of the utilization of truth.

The truth that humanity must collectively pursue must be truth that has real, constructive power. That truth must embrace the power of Oneness that can overcome differences in nationality, ethnicity, and religion. Such must be the nucleus of the Truth. However, a new and better world will not come about just because we recognize the Truth.

The Earth's environment will not renew itself overnight simply because we declare ourselves enlightened. Not just because we sing and dance in harmony and delight, will a spiritual civilization be born.

As with anything of lasting worth, an action plan needs to be formulated and acted on, with sincerity and fortitude. Truth must be actualized on Earth to have a lasting power. We must create a legacy of Truth through the transformation of our civilization. In this grand project, individual enlightenment has little meaning. Whole groups, organizations, and nations must become enlightened. Enlightenment must become common sense and Truth a matter of course. Only then will we herald the beginning of a spiritual civilization.

Creating a Beautiful World

I want to create a beautiful world. I love the earth that I was born into, and this is the only home possible for me. I know that my roots lie buried deep and inextricably inside the heart of the earth. I travel around the world in search of people who are willing to share my dreams and visions. I actually find many who share my thoughts and concerns, but often they find it very difficult to act upon these concerns. They allow fear of change, and inertia of the moment, to carry them further down the river. They are afraid to create a new world.

I began doing what I do 20 years ago in a small, local park in Central Korea. I still remember what I told my very first student. "Although you are one person today, you represent the whole of humanity standing in front of me. That's how precious you are to me." Although that person was somewhat perplexed at my admittedly grand statement, I had conviction that my efforts would have a deep and lasting impact on the future of humankind and the earth. The strength of my conviction has only increased since then.

I am still searching for more and more people who will engage in this grand project ... who will create the new spiritual-cultural revolution of the Earth-Human movement with me. We need a critical mass of one hundred million people. We need a strong community of one hundred million enlightened activists, Earth-Humans, to begin the process of breathing out. The first collective sigh of relief will not be a signal of capitulation, but of a new beginning, a new spiritual maturity. Humanity will have discovered the wisdom of breathing, the law of the cycle of life. Our breathing will be a sign our maturity.

It has been a long while since I slept more than three hours a night, not because I have superhuman strength, but because I have strength of vision. I cannot stop or pause until I have devoted my all to making my vision of a beautiful and peaceful earth into reality. I have carried this vision unchanged with me always, from a small park in Korea to where I am now, for this vision existed before anything that I have created since then. This vision is me ... my mind and my soul. This vision is my enlightenment and my salvation. I do not exist apart from this vision. I do not have a magical formula for solving all the problems that face us today. However, we have the power of the enlightened mind and awakened soul. This is enough to start. It is a good beginning.

To open a new era, we need more than vision and hope. We need an action plan. You cannot build a house by just wishing for one. To build a house, you first need land, architectural drawings, building materials, and skilled workers. Only when all these are ready can you begin construction of a house. Similarly, to construct a house of peace on Earth, you need a blueprint for peace, the required materials and skilled people to build it.

We need a step-by-step guide to building this house of peace. The first step is a vision for the creation of a peaceful Earth village, a true community for all human beings, a dream of a spiritual civilization. Combine this with the will, discipline, and fortitude to see this vision through or die trying, and you will have built the foundation for this house of peace.

The second step will consist of training people who are skilled enough to participate in the construction of this grand mansion. It will truly be the most magnificent mansion in the history of humankind. We need a program to train and graduate people, who not only share our vision, and add to the strength of our will, but who also bring skills and actual building know-how to the task at hand. The training program that I have created and systemized is called Dahnhak and Brain Respiration, in which people undergo an intimate, one-on-one experience of the energy of the Earth. Through this program they become Earth-Humans.

However, I am not beholden to any one system of training, even one of my own making. I am only interested in the result, the birth of a community, one hundred million strong, of Earth-Humans, skilled artisans in the construction of the 'Peace House.' The creation of these Earth-Humans is the third step in the process.

The fourth step in the building process is the formation of a worldwide alliance that will combine the strength of all Earth-Humans and coordinate their efforts. We can't have people trying to build this house separately. There needs to be organization and coordination. Otherwise, we may end up with a house with five bedrooms, but without any bathrooms, or with several dining rooms, but without a kitchen. I have called this alliance the "World Earth-Human Alliance."

Overcoming the problems we face today and planting the seed of peace is not a task for any one nation, people, or religion. This will only be possible when spiritually awakened people from every corner of the world share the power of a single vision and create an alliance of Earth-Humans. This alliance must not be an end in itself. Nothing happens just because you have incorporated an organization, appointed its directors, and adopted the by-laws. Nothing happens without a fundamental change in humans. Our habits, our thoughts, and our lives must change. Our human character must undergo a fundamental shift.

One hundred million is not a huge number. It is eminently doable. It is only one percent of the world's population, which is expected to crest to ten billion in twenty years. With only one percent of the human population, we will form the critical mass needed to begin the construction of peace. Peace in which every human being of every color, religion, and nationality can and will participate, with willingness and joy. Then we will have realized Mago's Dream.

A Gift of the Earth

I am honored and pleased to have had this opportunity to greet you through this book. This signifies that our paths have crossed and our souls have communed. As a token of my deepest appreciation, I would like to give you a most precious gift, a gift that you already possess but might not yet have realized. I would like to make a gift of the Earth.

Now, open your hands wide and lift them to your chest. Imagine the bright, blue-green Earth slowly descending from the air and settling gently upon your hands. Feel the Earth in your hands. Feel the energy of the

Earth. Feel your life energy reach for the Earth, mingling energy, and joyfully proclaiming your oneness. Feel the Earth in your hands become brighter, vibrating with joy and delight, transmitting this to you through your hands, arms, and heart.

Next, lift your hands, filled with the Earth, toward your head. Bring the Earth closer to your forehead. Feel the cool and comforting touch of the Earth on your forehead and gently and gradually guide the earth into your head. Inside your head, sense the spinning and vibrating of its' awesome vitality and energy. Feel the light of energy and life shine forth from your forehead as your energy and Earth's energy mingle in a dance of joyful oneness. You are now an Earth-Human, for you have just experienced Oneness with the Earth. How can you be anything less? You now have no choice but to express your love for the Earth, because it will be an expression of self-love. You are now a self appointed protector, keeper, and guardian of the Earth because you realize that your journey of self-discovery and spiritual completion begins and ends with the Earth. You are a child of the Earth.

Just imagine, ... one hundred million people with the Earth beating its blue-green light of life in their hearts.

Imagine one hundred million Earth-Humans. And imagine what we can do with the power of such awareness, and will ... a spiritual civilization come true. Imagine our luck. Imagine our blessing, to be blessed with a divine opportunity to participate in building this grand house of peace. It only comes once in many lifetimes. Let us make the best of it together.

Prayer of Peace

Ilchi Lee's prayer at the Opening Ceremony of the Millennium World Peace Summit of Religious and Spiritual Leaders in the General Assembly of the United Nations on August 28th, 2000.

I offer this prayer of peace
Not to any one god nor to many gods
Not only to the Christian god
Nor only to the Jewish god
Nor only the Buddhist god

Nor only the Islamic god

And not even to the indigenous gods of many nations

But to the divinity within that we all hold inside

That makes us all brothers and sisters

To make us truly a One Family

In the name of humanity.

I offer this prayer of peace

To the cosmic Oneness that is our birthright

And our privilege

And our strength

That should we let it shine and show us the way

Will guide us to the road of peace

Not the Christian peace

Not the Jewish peace

Not the Islamic peace

Nor the Buddhist peace

And not even the indigenous peace of many nations

But the human peace

That has a place in the hearts of all people

To allow us to truly fulfill our divine potential

To become the children of one humanity.

I offer this prayer of peace
To allow us all to realize
The truth of our existence
To allow us all to discover
The sanctity of our lives
To allow us to all to seek
The spirituality of our beings
Please allow us to experience
With all our hearts and our souls
The intimate connection to the divine
That we all posses inside
For our bodies are the temples of worship
And our souls the altars
Upon which we shall stand tall
And live out the true meaning
Of our existence.

I offer this prayer of peace
To declare a revolution
Of the human spirit
I wish to announce that
It is now time
For all of us to spiritually awaken

And become enlightened

That the time for the enlightened few is over

That the age of elitist enlightenment has passed

For how long do you seek to wait for prophets

To come down from mountaintops

And tell us what to do

We all must become enlightened

To recognize our divinity

To raise up our consciousness

And proclaim our independence

From blind reliance on long ago sages

And find the answers from our own well

Of spiritual wisdom

We must ourselves become the enlightened ones

We must ourselves realize our Oneness

I declare that we must all become "earthlings"

Of the earth

And not of any religion, nation, or race.

But of this earth, for this earth, and by this earth

To create a lasting peace

On earth.

I offer this prayer of peace

With all my fellow "Earth-Humans"
For a lasting peace on earth.

Humanity Conference - Declaration of Humanity

World-renowned scholars, thinkers and social activists came together in Seoul, Korea on June 15, 2001 to attend the First Annual 'New Millennium World Peace and Humanity Conference.' They met to explore ideas concerning the concrete influence that spirituality can have on our current political, economic and cultural makeup.

The New Millennium Peace Foundation is a non-governmental, independent organization, founded in 1997 by Dr. Ilchi Lee and Neale Donald Walsch. Invited guests included prestigious academicians, journalists, activists, and experts in the fields of religion, journalism, culture, environment and most importantly, human potential. Distinguished guests included; Dr. Ilchi Lee, president of the NMPF and co-host of the conference, and Neale Donald Walsch, co-host and the world's best selling author of the 'Conversations with God' series and founder of the 'ReCreation Foundation'. Other honored guests were: Maurice Strong, senior advisor to the Secretary General of the United Nations and president of the United Nations University for Peace; Seymour Topping, administrator of the Pulitzer Prize and professor of international journalism at Columbia University Graduate School of Journalism; Reverend Wyatt Tee Walker, senior pastor of Canaan Baptist Church, noted civil rights activist and former executive secretary to Martin Luther King; Jean Houston, world's leading researcher on human potential and co-director of the Foundation for Mind Research; Hanne Strong, president of Manitou Foundation and an environmental activist; and Audrey Ronning Topping, a Pulitzer prize winning photo-journalist and author. The keynote speaker was former U.S. vice-president Al Gore, recently a visiting professor at Columbia University Graduate School of Journalism.

The conference resulted in the adoption of the historic

'Declaration of Humanity', a brief document that can be described as the Magna Carta for the Earth and Earth-Humans, whose highest common identity is that of one who has transcended the artificial boundaries of nation-hood, religion, and ethnicity to become a citizen of the Earth. This document was adopted officially by the special guests, conference participants and more than 12,000 enthusiastic Earth-Humans. There was much fanfare and joy. Thus far, more than 100,000 people have signed on. Here is the full text of the Declaration of Humanity:

Declaration of Humanity (June 15th, 2001)

1. I declare that I am a spiritual being, an essential and eternal part of the Soul of Humanity, one and indivisible.

2. I declare that I am a human being, whose rights and security ultimately depend on assuring the human rights of all people of Earth.

3. I declare that I am a child of the earth, with the will and awareness to work for goals that benefit the entire community of life on Earth.

4. I declare that I am a healer, with the power and

purpose to heal the many forms of divisions and conflicts that exist on Earth.

5. I declare that I am a protector, with the knowledge and responsibility to help the Earth recover her natural harmony and beauty.

6. I declare that I am an activist in service to the world, with the commitment and the ability to make a positive difference in my society.

If you would like to sign your name to show support and agreement, please visit www.healingsociety.org

Hill Top in Sedona Mago Garden

Songs of
Sedona Mago Garden

As morning sun graces Sedona Mago Garden,
Red soil awakens to her calling
And birds noisily greet the dawn.

As zephyr stirs across the tree tops,
Leaves and grasses dance to the voices
Of Mother Earth whispering her love.

As evening sun sets on Sedona Mago Garden,
Secret Mountain yonder beckons with an embrace
Rejoicing in the golden, sacred light.

As stars twinkle above Sedona Mago Garden,
She merges into the eternal Nothingness
Drawing sacred beauty not of this world.

As moon glows upon Sedona Mago Garden,
Trees, lakes, and all life sing and dance in thanks
Inside the grandest spotlight of all.

Sedona Mago Garden houses three canyons
Chunhwa, Mago, and Senya;
Sedona Mago Garden hides three caves
Chunhwa, Mago, and Dangun;
Sedona Mago Garden embraces one lake
Dangun's Lake;
Sedona Mago Garden hosts twelve vortices.

Sedona Mago Garden veils that most sacred place of
    all
The Garden of Gods above Chunhwa Canyon.
A magical place where gods talk and plan of peace
Sending forth the divine energy
To awaken the souls in Sedona Mago Garden.

Sedona Mago Garden is the home
To people working to realize human health and peace
    healers.

As flowers cover the Earth with their beauty,
Let the power of the spiritual movement,
Let the healing energy of the Vortices
Radiate from Sedona Mago Garden
And cover the world.

SUN waits for us there
100 million strong healing community
Becoming one with Mother Earth
There lies our vision and dreams.

The first upon this Earth
A school to teach the Law of Heavenly Ascension
    (Chunhwa)
Path to divine healing on earth

They are coming to Sedona Mago Garden
With dreams of healers
With dreams of peace

With Mago's Dreams
To love humanity and the Earth
They are coming to Sedona Mago Garden.

Our dreams
Mago's Dreams
Are One
And the same.

Mago's Dream will come true
Through Peace of the Power Brain.

Even today
A new day dawns
With joyous shouts and greetings
Of Mago's healers.

Ilchi Lee's Other Books

Healing Society
: A Prescription for Global Enlightenment
A simple yet groundbreaking explanation of enlightenment, Healing Society proclaims an enlightenment revolution in which enlightenment is no longer reserved for a select few, but the birthright of all. "Enlightenment is choice", it proclaims. This is the first book by a Korean born author ever to reach #1 on Amazon.com.

The 12 Enlightenments for Healing Society(June, 2002)
The long awaited sequel to *Healing Society*. In twelve profound chapters, it makes accessible, in an easy and flowing style, the often-complex topics of spirituality and questions of existence. Through 12 distinct but interconnected enlightenments, you will learn the why's and how's of healing individuals, society, and the earth.

Peaceology for Healing Society (Spring, 2003)

As one of the most renowned spiritual teachers of his age, the author outlines the philosophy of peace that places the earth as the central standard of value around which the world can rally to overcome the ethnic, national, and religions obstacles to peace. "Peace is breathing," he states and compares peace to the natural rhythm of life, as indispensable to human living as breathing and eating. Peaceology is a living peace created through action, not a static dream made of words and thoughts.

Brain Respiration: Making Your Brain Creative, Peaceful, and Productive (August, 2002)

This is the amazing result of combining body-mind-spirit training with the latest in scientific brain research. Brain Respiration, a revolutionary method to awaken the brain to its fullest potential, creates not only a powerful but also a peaceful, creative, and productive brain for the 21st Century. Exercise the brain by breathing with the cosmic energy. Learn to develop 100% of the potential of the brain by utilizing the power of the natural rhythm of life within you.